Routledge Revivals

Writing for Television

This book, first published in 1955, was written at the request of the BBC in an attempt to help the professional writer to take advantage of the opportunities offered by the television medium. This title will be of interest to students of history, literature and media studies, and will also appeal to the general reader who is interested in knowing how television programmes were constructed.

I0880966

Writing for Television

Basil Bartlett

Routledge
Taylor & Francis Group
ROUTLEDGE REVIVALS

First published in 1955
by George Allen & Unwin Ltd

This edition first published in 2015 by Routledge
2 Park Square, Milton Park, Abingdon, Oxon, OX14 4RN
and by Routledge
711 Third Avenue, New York, NY 10017

Routledge is an imprint of the Taylor & Francis Group, an informa business

© 1955 George Allen & Unwin Ltd

All rights reserved. No part of this book may be reprinted or reproduced or utilised in any form or by any electronic, mechanical, or other means, now known or hereafter invented, including photocopying and recording, or in any information storage or retrieval system, without permission in writing from the publishers.

Publisher's Note

The publisher has gone to great lengths to ensure the quality of this reprint but points out that some imperfections in the original copies may be apparent.

Disclaimer

The publisher has made every effort to trace copyright holders and welcomes correspondence from those they have been unable to contact.

A Library of Congress record exists under LC control number: 57000515

ISBN 13: 978-1-138-12351-9 (hbk)
ISBN 13: 978-1-315-64869-9 (ebk)
ISBN 13: 978-1-138-12370-0 (pbk)

Writing for Television

by

Sir Basil Bartlett, Bt.

Formerly Drama Script Supervisor
BBC Television Service

London

George Allen & Unwin Ltd

Ruskin House Museum Street

First published in 1955
This book is copyright under the Berne Convention. Apart from any fair dealing for the purposes of private study, research, criticism or review, as permitted under the Copyright Act 1911, no portion may be reproduced by any process without written permission. Enquiry should be made to the publisher.

© George Allen & Unwin Ltd, 1955

Printed in Great Britain
in 12 point Pilgrim type
by Simson Shand Ltd
London Hertford and Harlow

TO MY WIFE

Miss Mary Malcolm

Contents

Introduction

I HAVE written this little book for the professional writer. I hope that it may be of use to him.

Television, whether we like it or not, has come to stay. Television aerials are springing up all over the country, and it is quite certain that, in the future, practically every family in Great Britain will come to depend, in some way or other, on the Television Services for its news, sport, enlightenment and entertainment.

It is not within my competence to assess the overall contribution which Television can make to the life of the nation. All I am concerned with here is the author. And all I have tried to do is give him a few hints, in the hope that they will help him to take advantage of the tremendous opportunities offered him by the new medium.

A great many authors would like to write for Television, but do not know how to set about it. 'What does the BBC want from us?' they ask. 'What sort of writing? In what form? How much is it prepared to pay? How are programmes planned? How are plays produced? What happens in the studio? Is there a closed shop? Do we have to go back to school and learn a whole lot of new abracadabra before our work will be considered? Is it worth our while? It is all very mysterious and a bit beyond our comprehension. Surely we fit in somewhere!'

These are all reasonable questions. And I have done my best to answer them.

I should like to begin by assuring authors that there is nothing mysterious about Television. In order to write for the Television medium, it is unnecessary for them to have been born in a Television studio, queer products of boom-operators out of vision-mixers. Any author, whatever his background, can turn himself quite easily into a Television writer provided that he uses his commonsense and is prepared to study the medium. Commonsense is the important thing.

The would-be Television writer will, of course, have a lot to learn. He must study scripting and costing and production methods. He must watch rehearsals and, when his plays are produced, must study them from the gallery of a studio. He must see for himself what the cameras can do and how much he can expect from actors. He must, in fact, learn an entirely new craft.

If he is serious about all this and thinks it worth his while, he will find that the BBC will help. There is at the moment only a handful of writers experienced in Television technique. In time, no doubt, a whole generation of pure Television writers will emerge. Meanwhile, in this interim period, the BBC is only too anxious to encourage authors who have already made their mark in other forms of writing to turn their attention to the new medium. There is no closed shop. The BBC doors are open to everyone.

One thing the BBC cannot do. It cannot teach writers how to write. That is why I have said that this book is intended for professionals. I do not mean to be harsh on amateurs. After all, what is an amateur but a would-be professional who has not yet learned his job? But I do not see how amateurs can compete with professionals in programmes which are already National and may soon be European if not Universal.

Chapter I

Television and other Mediums

FIRST, a short survey.

I

BASICALLY, Television is a by-product of the theatre. Just as the cinema turned to the legitimate theatre for its actors so does Television turn above all to the theatre for its writers. And the author already experienced in the ways of the theatre is the author most likely to be able to make the mental adjustment necessary for the Television medium.

Television requires of an author much the same discipline as does the theatre. It asks him to tell a story. And it asks him to tell it by means of credible and interesting characters, into whose mouths he has put dialogue which rings true and which conveys his meaning clearly. That is the basis of a Television play just as it is the basis of a theatre play. It is also the basis of serials, series and adaptations.

In many ways Television is less exacting than the theatre. It can, for example, take short cuts which are impossible in the theatre. It can move from set to set and from actor to actor less ponderously than can the theatre. And it does not give the author the same problems of sustaining interest through long scenes and devising ingenious exits and entrances for his characters. Most important of all, its cameras can give emphasis in close-up to certain dramatic moments in the action more easily than is possible on the stage. Indeed, on Television, a visual image can often take the place of what, in the theatre, can only be expressed by a series of speeches.

As a natural corollary to this a playwright will find that he needs much less dialogue on Television than he needed in the theatre. Pictures tell a lot of his story for him.

On Television there is no time limit to his play. He can write his story just as he feels it, giving it the exact number of minutes it requires. He is not forced to lengthen it artificially to suit managements who insist that it should run for two hours, with breaks at specified times, and that the number of its sets should be limited.

Subject to the restrictions of the studio a Television writer can set his scenes more or less where he pleases. This does not mean that he should set them all over the world. If he does, his play will become confused and incoherent. But it does mean that he can jump quite easily from the drawing-room to the bathroom and back again without worrying about the scene-changing difficulties with which he would be confronting the stage-management of a theatre.

He can rely, too, on more facial expression from his actors. The Television screen is small but, in that small screen, faces can be shown very large. On the other hand he must remember that Television actors haven't any feet. At least they show their feet only when the script specifically requires them to do so. And, when they have feet, the chances are that they will not have faces. At moments of crisis the Television dramatist will have to choose between feet and faces.

II

I HAVE deliberately emphasized the importance to

Television of the theatre because so many people seem to think that a Television play is just a potted film. This is far from true. Technically Television does, of course, owe a lot to the cinema. A Television play is produced in a studio, not in a theatre. Its scenes are photographed by cameras and projected on to screens. It may actually have cut into it, from time to time, many hundreds of feet of film. And captions, close-ups, fades, sound-tracks and superimpositions are only a few of the words which Television has borrowed from the film vocabulary. But the whole approach of Television is different from that of the cinema.

A film, after all, is a mosaic, its pieces carefully blended together in the cutting-room. It may take months to shoot. It may be photographed in a hundred varying locations, in all sorts of weather and in no coherent order. Each of its scenes may be viewed by the camera from a dozen different angles before the perfect picture emerges.

A Television play, on the other hand, is live, continuous, consecutive. Its only cutting-room is in its director's head. The director may have as many as five hundred camera changes in his script. Each one must have been carefully and correctly planned in advance. For, once the play begins, it cannot stop. Actors may dry. Lights may fuse. Sound may fade. Cameras may peel. Flats may fall down. The calamities that may happen to a director are unlimited. He can only pray and, to a certain extent, improvise. In dire extremity he can abandon the whole thing and flash on to his screen a notice saying that there has been a mechanical breakdown. When he does that, he knows that he may well have broken the spell of his play and may never retrieve it.

That is the way of the theatre, not of the cinema. For

stage plays and Television plays are living things, whereas films are in cans.

III

ALL the same, the screenwriter has a great deal to contribute to the development of Television. His experience in films will have taught him, for example, how to illustrate his story with pictures and how to tell it in a straight, continuous line, not breaking it up for intervals and visits to the bar. He will also have learned how to capture an audience's attention. The playwright knows that he need not hurry with his opening scenes. His audience will be quite content to let him spend a quarter of an hour setting his characters before propelling them slowly into the action. A film audience is far more impatient. It expects the story to begin as soon as the captions are over. In the same way a Television viewer is apt to switch off if a Television story does not immediately grip him.

What will bother the screenwriter in Television is its roughness, its lack of external resources, its dependence on a small number of actors and inexpensive sets, and the fact that it is continuous. He will miss the leisureliness, the opulence, the polish of the films.

On the other hand he will appreciate the status he has as a writer. The cinema may pay him large sums of money. In return it usually takes away from him the full control of his story. He frequently has to sit back and watch it torn to pieces by directors, producers, actors and other writers, to say nothing of distributors. On Television—at least on BBC Television—the standards of the theatre prevail. Once an author's work has been accepted it becomes the sole purpose of the director, actors and technicians to see that it is projected as well as is humanly feasible on to the screen. No one has to worry about the feelings of stars, the box-office or the dollar situation. Television respects the author's integrity.

IV

THE novelist, when approaching Television, may have to revolutionize his way of thinking. His work is meant to be read, not seen or heard. And it will be hard for him to narrow his vision down to Television terms. Some novelists claim to see their work in pictures. If that is true, they will probably find that many of their pictures are difficult to realize with Television cameras. In addition, they will almost certainly have to learn to write actable dialogue.

What the novelist has to offer are his imagination, and his characters, which are often more deeply observed than those of the playwright or screenwriter. His greatest advantage will be that he does not normally write for an audience, but for a single reader.

The short-story writer is a natural for Television. The attack, precision and economy required of him in his normal work should make it easy for him to write the short, anecdotal plays so badly needed in Television programmes.

V

IN some ways the medium furthest removed from Television is Sound Radio. Writing for Sound has been developed into a considerable art. But it is an art with quite different objectives, an evocative art, one that plays with words and rhythms, creating illusions, conjuring up pictures in the imagination. A Sound writer is not concerned with the practical problems that face Television. He does not have to worry about costume, make-up, sets or budgets. He has, in fact, practically no production difficulties at all. He can travel at will all over the world, and backwards and forwards in time. And his continuity can be held together for him by a narrator. He can make a character say: 'Look. There are a hundred and fifty thousand people coming up the drive.' And, if he says so, his listeners will believe that it is true. He will have shocks coming to him when he turns his attention to Television.

All the same, the Radio writer's experience with sound can be adapted very profitably to Television, where, in the excitement of discovering pictures, most people are apt to forget the enormous power of words and, in particular, of music. Once the Sound writer has mastered the technique of Television he will be able to contribute great things to the Sound track, which can be so designed as to heighten and point the action of a story or, alternatively, can be used contrapuntally.

VI

IN a word, Television will have a different impact on different kinds of writers. Some will chafe under its restrictions. Others will marvel at the opportunities it offers. What is certain is that Television is still a comparatively new world. Existing programmes are only a prelude to what will happen tomorrow. The future of the medium lies in the minds and imaginations of writers.

VII

ALL considerations of technique apart, the Television writer is faced with only one problem. It is a new problem and it is vital. It is the problem of the tiny screen and the single viewer. Once he has solved that he has solved everything.

Chapter II

Choice of Subject

I

THE author will ask, what are the most suitable subjects for Television?

I find this a hard question to answer. Almost any subject is suitable provided that it is properly handled. The treatment of a subject, as a general rule, is of far greater importance than the subject itself.

The BBC does, of course, make certain reservations in its choice of subject. Although not liable to censorship by the Lord Chamberlain it is compelled, by the nature of its Charter, to exercise a strict internal censorship of its own. This amounts to no more than a sense of responsibility for what is shown to the family and seen in the home. Thus there is no place in BBC programmes for plays that might normally be produced in private theatre clubs. And any author who has an urge to write a play on a distasteful theme—rape, for example, or incest or abortion—would be better advised not to write it for Television.

The BBC must also be cautious about plays with a strong political content. This does not mean that political plays are never produced. But it does mean that the Television screen cannot be used by the playwright as a political platform.

In addition, there is a quite natural ban on the portrayal of the Royal Family in fictional programmes.

Apart from these few commonsense restrictions I

doubt if there are any subjects at all which cannot be considered for Television production. Plays are judged on their dramatic merit, and an outstanding play by any author, old or new, will always be given serious consideration. There may, from time to time, be delays in production. An expensive play, for example, may require a special budget. And one aimed specifically at a minority audience may have to wait a little while before finding its place in the schedule.

II

TO be on the safe side an author, before settling down to write a play for Television, should first submit a synopsis. This should be in short story form and should run to not more than one thousand words. If the author is new to Television he should also submit a few pages of specimen dialogue as a general guide to the style and quality of his writing.

I do not personally care very much for synopses. And I know that many authors hate them. But they have their value. They enable the BBC to tell an author if his subject matter is on the danger list, or if it is covered by another play already in the planning stage of production. It is surprising how often a number of authors hit on the same theme at the same time. It is usually difficult to give an unqualified 'yes' to a synopsis. But a red light at an early stage may often save an author a lot of unnecessary labour.

Of course, no author with an insistent theme in his head will be deterred from writing it by Cassandra croaks from me or from anyone else. That is as it should be. And good luck to him.

III

WHILE reading plays submitted for Television production I have been struck by certain mistakes quite regularly made. It may be of help if I refer to them.

To begin with, a great many writers tend to write beyond the range of their experience. The results are usually fatal. A man's own life may seem to him dull. To others it may be fascinating. And he is far more likely to write a good play if he sticks to characters he knows and situations with which he is familiar than by launching out into an alien environment. This applies at all levels. An Oxford Don is no better qualified to write a play about the Bowery than is an Australian boundary-rider to write a drawing-room comedy. Writing a play is difficult enough as it is. It seems sheer folly for an author to tackle a subject about which he knows nothing. This is a criticism, I know, that can be levelled at playwrights and novelists just as well as at Television writers. But somehow ignorance, inaccuracy and insincerity are more disturbing when shown up by the Television camera than almost anywhere else.

Another odd mistake that authors make is in thinking that history has provided us all with cast iron plots and personalities which need only to be fitted out with dialogue to become masterpieces. I do not say that all historical plays are bad. Far from it. But an author should ask himself whether his imagination has really been fired by one special historical story or whether he lacks invention. He should remember, too, that most of the outstanding historical stories have already been done to death by other and possibly more skilful writers. A good historical play can, of course, be very popular. There is a strong element of dressing-up in the theatre, and most English actors, in spite of their great reputation for playing modern comedy, enjoy costume and like to identify themselves with the heroes and heroines of the past. All the same, an author must be quite sure that his historical story will stand on its own feet as a story even when stripped of its historical trappings. He may be a good scholar himself and have steeped himself in a particular period. None of that work will help him at all if his story and characters are not dramatically sound. And, of course, he can rely on no co-operation whatever from the viewers.

The natural good sense of authors should keep them clear of other unpromising subjects. The BBC is, on the whole, more adventurous than most theatre managements. But even the BBC is not going to allow an author to ride his private hobby-horse to death at the expense of the public. Plays packed full of symbolism, for example, plays about the ancient gods, or long, expensive chronicle plays will probably meet with the same cool reception at the BBC as anywhere else. And I should, I suppose, at this moment put out the usual warnings against fantasy, although I have a feeling that, in the future, magic of all kinds will bring tremendous opportunities to the Television cameras.

Pretentious plays of any kind are even more disastrous on Television than in the theatre. Nothing is more dismal than an unsuccessful so-called highbrow play.

One tip. The Television writer should be a little cautious about plays in dialect. Although the BBC has regional responsibilities its programme is a national one, and authors should remember that dialect falls strangely on the ordinary ear. What pleases in Belfast, Cardiff or Aberdeen may be quite incomprehensible to other inhabitants of these islands. No author need feel discouraged from writing in his own idiom. But he should bear in mind that the broader his play the less likely it is to be acceptable to the general public.

Finally, satire.

Many authors revel in writing satire. On Television they will have to curb themselves. Perhaps we are all of us a little sensitive and insecure just now. In the past—with Fielding, Swift and Pope—we had a great tradition of savage satire in this country. And solid societies like the Late Victorians could afford to be good-humoured when bricks were thrown at them. But nowadays all sorts of people—doctors, lawyers, Anglican priests—seem to take even the gentlest satire as a personal attack on their integrity. And the viewers support them. If an author wishes to write satire for Television he must disguise it. A gentle wind of satire blowing through a play will probably pass unnoticed by the many, but will delight the few.

IV

I SEEM so far to have written nothing but 'don'ts'.

On the positive side, there is an overwhelming need for comedies of every description. Although Television viewers are prepared at times to be harrowed, moved or even uplifted, what they normally expect is to be entertained. And the supply of good comedies can never keep pace with the demand. Comedy writing is a most difficult art, and very few comedies survive their generation. They are like newspapers, absorbing on the day of publication, but very soon dead. Manners change so quickly. Morality, the Law even, alters its emphasis, and what amuses today may seem terribly dull tomorrow. As a result, a well-made comedy is a valuable property, eagerly sought after by Television as well as by film companies and by theatrical managements. The problem facing the BBC is that it gets through comedies at such a tremendous rate. A comedy which fills a theatre for two years is exhausted on Television after two performances. And whereas a West End manager can make a handsome fortune out of two or three comedies, the BBC can scarcely keep the wolf from the door with fifty. To authors who are wondering what subjects will be given preference by the BBC I can only say that good comedies are always most welcome but that they are very hard to write.

In the past, farce has proved unplayable on Television. The demands made on actors were too great. Comedy is, after all, a matter of dialogue, and good dialogue comes across in any medium, whereas farce depends on business, and business requires the co-operation of an audience. Fortunately the BBC now has its own theatre at Shepherd's Bush and is also equipped to give Outside Broadcasts from other theatres. As a result, farce can at last be played with some hope of approbation before an invited audience.

This is true of melodrama also, but to a limited extent. The extravagance of melodrama is not really suited to the Television medium.

Next in popularity to comedies are whodunits. A whodunit is, of course, a mathematical exercise. For Television it must not be too brutal because of the children, although, as we all know, children are far more bloodthirsty than grown-up people. It must be plausible but must not probe too deeply into human relationships. It must be workmanlike, preferably witty, and must retain throughout an element of suspense.

There remain the Human Story and what I can only describe as the Well-Made Play, in which the story goes driving along, with good strong parts for leading actors. These are the eternal standbys of the theatre in all its many forms.

V

AS a very general rule I might add that plays with a plot are more suitable for Television than plays of atmosphere. A mood is always hard to set and maintain, whereas it is comparatively easy to produce a play in which the viewers are continually asking themselves: 'What happens next?'

There are, of course, a hundred exceptions to this as to every rule. Authors are constantly writing plays on the most improbable subjects and getting away with them. And an author with a really original line of thought should work it for all it is worth. He should never let himself be influenced by what has happened to the efforts of other people. The author who hopes for success by imitating the successful work of other authors is usually disappointed.

Chapter III

The Viewers

HAVING decided on the subject of his play, the Television writer must consider how best he can present it to the viewers.

I

EVERY author with a sense of self-preservation pays close attention to the likes and dislikes of his public. A few authors write for themselves alone, defying the taste of their contemporaries. Fewer still, and these the greatest, have managed, more by chance than by design, to overcome the limitations of their environment and have written for all ages and for all classes of mankind. But the normal author is the servant of his public, delighted with its approval, hurt and puzzled by its displeasure.

I have a suspicion that many authors of the past must have found the conventions in which they were forced to write extremely irksome. Did Aeschylus, for example, enjoy hearing his lines declaimed by actors on stilts and wearing masks? Or did Racine of his own free will squeeze his stories into Alexandrines? They wrote as they did because their patrons demanded it of them.

In our own theatrical history playwrights have had to do many unpalatable things. The Restoration dramatists, for example, in order to make a living, had to write lewd comedies to please a coterie of gallants, newly emancipated from a Puritan dictatorship. And those most Philistine of our ancestors, the Edwardians, who appear to have regarded the theatre as a means of getting through the awkward periods between dinner and supper, expected their authors to write plays in five acts, the first immaterial because the audience had not yet arrived, the fifth superfluous because the audience had already departed. Nearer home, our peculiar licensing laws have caused playwrights to bring down their second act curtains early so that their patrons would not miss the bars. Such frivolous considerations as these have often determined the structure, even the content, of a play.

But playwrights are adaptable people. They have to be. For they know that a play on the shelf is a dead thing and that they will lose their livelihood unless they please their patrons

The Television writer is no exception. On Television the public continues to pay the piper and, in consequence, calls the tune.

II

ONE of the biggest problems facing the Television writer is that his public is so elusive. The playwright has at least always known what his public looked like and what it wanted. If he was in any doubt, there have been boos and rotten eggs and empty benches to remind him. Even the screenwriter, although he does not work through flesh-and-blood actors, can watch the reactions of his audience as it is gathered together in a picture house. And both have the ultimate test of the box-office. The Television writer, on the other hand, is writing in a vacuum. He has a potential public of many millions. But he can never be sure, at any given moment, that those millions have not switched off. For all he knows they may not be watching his play at all, but be quietly playing cards or drinking tea in the kitchen. As a result, every line he writes is an act of faith. The old convention that the audience is part of the play does not apply to him.

Indeed he has not, in the accepted sense of the word, any audience at all. Instead, he has a multitude of viewers, who watch his work either singly or in very small groups. This is an entirely new situation for a dramatic author. In order to meet it he must learn not only a new technique but a new point of view.

What writing for Television really means is that the author is trying to tell a story to a single individual, who is not obliged to listen to it, who has not paid for his seat, whose attention must be well and firmly held if he is not going to switch off his set. All questions of technique dwindle before this one important fact. It decides the whole conception of the author's play.

III

WHO then is the viewer? And what does he want?

The answers to these two questions are simple. The viewer is the average man. And what he wants is to be told a story which he can both enjoy and understand. If it is true that an author should not write beyond the range of his experience, it is equally true that he should not write beyond the experience of the viewer. This does not mean that he should write down to him. Woe betide him if he does. The viewer dislikes having his intelligence insulted. But he must also be careful not to write above his head. He must remember that there is no snobbery among viewers as there so often is among theatre audiences. The viewer makes up his own mind about a play. His judgement is not affected by the reactions of his neighbours to the right and left of him. And he is no respecter of reputations.

In addition, the majority of viewers have no theatrical background. Many of them have never been in a theatre in their lives. They come to the screen unprejudiced and uninformed. They have no mental yardstick by which to judge a play.

IV

WITH these considerations in mind the Television writer should write his play in a simple, sincere and intelligible way. He will be quite safe if he chooses a familiar theme and works it out in dialogue which the viewers can understand and by means of characters with whose outlook they can identify themselves. This sounds bald. And I do not wish to imply that the viewers are morons. There are, after all, many witty and moving variations to be written on the themes of 'Robin Hood' and 'Cinderella'. But the viewer is easily puzzled. And, when he is puzzled, he becomes resentful. The only way to hold his attention is to treat him gently and gain his confidence.

If the author wishes to tell an unusual story, he must proceed more carefully. He must put up signposts now and then to show the viewer exactly where he is going. Thus an unusual story is best told in terms of recognizable characters. And unusual characters are best set against a background which is familiar. If the author wishes to tell a story which is both unusual in itself and also filled with unusual characters he is taking a big risk. In the short time at his disposal it is doubtful whether he will be able to do both these things and still keep the viewers with him.

If he decides to throw caution to the winds and write deliberately for a minority audience, for the hard core of better-educated viewers, he must remember that the BBC Television Service puts out a single programme and that the time allotted to minorities is considerably less than is possible, for example, on Sound radio, which has three channels. And the competition for the few minority spaces on Television is a stiff one.

V

WHATEVER theme the author has chosen, and however he proposes to handle it, he must first be clear about his story line. This is most important. If his story line gets lost his play will fail. It is immaterial how many sets he uses or how many characters. His whole story may fit into a single set. Or it may spread out into several. What matters is that each scene should follow logically after the scene before and that each scene should carry the story forward. It is here that the playwright's theatre discipline will help him. Television has many temptations. It gives the author frequent opportunities of breaking his story line. He can, for example, use asides. By this I mean that he can play short scenes on film or in odd corners. These devices are perfectly legitimate provided always that they really help the story on its way. Television technique is there to point the story, not to confuse it. And Television technical facilities are no more than a snare if the author uses them as amusing tricks and forgets that it is his primary business to tell a story.

When he forgets his story it is probable that he will also have forgotten the viewer to whom he is telling it.

VI

I MIGHT add that, if the author takes a little trouble, he will not find the viewer hard to please. The viewer, if mishandled, can be resentful. But, if properly approached, alone, relaxed and comfortable in his own armchair, he is a sitting bird. And, once a true contact has been made with him, the impact of the author's mind on his can be terrific, in my opinion greater than anything that can be achieved in any other medium.

VII

FINALLY, a word or two about those most persistent of all viewers, the critics.

Television criticism, although abundant, can be very misleading. Television critics have to cover a great variety of programmes and cannot hope to be expert in all subjects. So far as original plays are concerned, they are up against a major difficulty in that there is as yet no 'Dramaturgie' for Television. In the theatre there are rules which are known instinctively to everyone. One stage play can be measured against another, a new author against an old, a new technique against a tried one. On Television almost everything is happening for the very first time.

On the whole the best Television critics are several jumps ahead of the ordinary viewer in taste and judgement. As a result, they tend to miscalculate what the viewers enjoy. Indeed, the more intelligent a critic happens to be, the more likely he is to overestimate the experience of the viewers. As time goes on, the critical powers of the viewers will improve. The more plays they see the more accurately will they be able to judge what is good of its own kind, whether tragedy, comedy or bedroom farce.

Meanwhile the critic can do no more than back his own particular fancy, without rules, without benefit of an audience response and without helpful tips from colleagues. And the author may take some consolation from the fact that, when the critic is in doubt about the virtues of a play, he is liable to give it a far worse notice than it deserves. It is, after all, more creditable to be the only man who has failed to appreciate a good play than it is to be the only man who has praised a bad one.

Chapter IV

The Layout of a Television Play

I

A TELEVISION writer should be competent to write a camera script. Until he can do so he is not entitled to call himself a Television writer.

In his first attempts, however, an author should not worry his head too much about cameras. He should content himself with blocking out his story in master scenes with full dialogue and a full description of his characters and action. He can safely leave the technical side to the BBC directors who are accustomed to making their own camera scripts with little or no help at all from the author.

A Television camera script resembles the final shooting script of a film. It is divided into two columns. In the left-hand column go the pictures and the camera directions. In the right-hand column goes the dialogue. The Americans call these two columns 'video' and 'audio'. A camera script is written on foolscap paper, and one page of foolscap, unless there are long speeches, is calculated to run about a minute and a quarter.

An experienced Television writer will write a very full left-hand column, giving the director every possible indication of how he wants his story presented. A less experienced writer should leave his left-hand column fairly blank, although he is, of course, at liberty to scribble notes in it if he has envisaged particular close-ups or camera movements. But he should remember that, until he knows his job, his camera directions will be less than useless. The BBC would far rather have a plain tale plainly told than a complicated camera script written by an author suffering from an attack of technology.

Even an experienced Television writer will hesitate to write a full camera script until he knows which director is going to direct his play. For directors' methods vary. Some, for example, favour fast cutting, whereas others prefer slow panning, and, although a good director can probably adapt his methods to suit the mood of his author, it is as well for an author to know how his director's mind is working if he wants the best results from him. This is, of course, a commonplace in the cinema where writers and directors invariably work together on a script.

There is no standard layout for a Television script. Some directors like a rehearsal script in which everything that concerns the actor is in the right-hand column. Others prefer the right-hand column to contain only dialogue. In any case, when rehearsals are under way, the left-hand column is peeled off and the director's final camera script or his modification of the author's camera script will take its place.

For information I might add that three cameras are normally allocated to a Television drama production and that a fourth is on call if required.

II

THE optimum length for a Television play is between sixty and ninety minutes, although plays can run longer or much shorter as the story demands. In the past the majority of BBC Television plays have been adaptations of theatre plays and, obviously, a well-made theatre play cannot be chopped down to much less than an hour and a half if it is to retain its essential structure. As a result, Television plays have tended to run for ninety to a hundred minutes or even longer. A Shakespeare play, for example, can scarcely run for less than two hours. And the British public, unlike the American, has grown accustomed to plays of this length. When writing specially for the Television medium, however, an author should remember that ninety minutes is a long time during which to hold the viewers' attention, even with intervals. And, unless he is quite unable to pack his story into a shorter time, he should aim at an hour or a little longer. Played through without a break, a play of this length holds the attention and does not strain the eyes.

There are also spots in the programme for much shorter plays. There is at present a dearth of suitable half-hour plays. When these come to be written I am sure that they will create their own demand.

III

NOW as to sets.

Theoretically an author may ask for as many sets as can be built in the studio. A normal studio will hold comfortably two or three main (three-walled) sets and a number of smaller (two-walled) sets which can be used for short scenes in or out of doors. In practice an author should be as economical as possible, for sets cost money, and an author making moderate demands for sets will be more likely to see his play produced than one requiring the earth. Anyway, the value of sets can be exaggerated. Television is an intimate medium, and the viewers are far more interested in the story which the author has to tell than in the background against which it is played. It is impossible, of course, to generalize in these matters. BBC designers are extremely gifted, and a fine setting can often make all the difference to a play. And an author need not be afraid to ask for special settings even though it may not always be possible to give him exactly what he wants. But he should remember that a single set has far more variety on Television than in the theatre where it is always seen from the same angle. An ingenious director, with clever lighting and clever camera work, can make a single set look like six. And there are very many excellent Television plays which can be produced without any sets at all, the director relying entirely on lighting, drapes and a few props for his effects. Here the author must use his commonsense. I should advise him to worry no more about sets than he does about camera angles, merely bearing in mind that economy is prudent and that some of the most skilful Television writers manage to get by triumphantly with a minimum of demands on the Design and Supply Department. If the play needs opening out, the author can ask for back projection slides, which give the illusion of sets without the sets being actually built. The author will discover for himself the value and the snags of BP when he comes to work in the studio. For the time being I think it would be safer to say that the use of BP should be left to the discretion of the director.

In his efforts to compress a play into a single set, the author should not forget that Television sets are more elastic than theatre sets. The camera, for example, can look out of the window of a Television set in a way that is not possible in the theatre. And, if the characters see people playing tennis in the garden, there is no earthly reason why the camera should not go nosing out and see them too. A stage convention allows characters to describe what is going on off stage. Television prefers to see for itself. 'Father is upstairs shaving' is normal theatre. Television cuts the line and shows a picture.

Similarly, the reaction in close-up of one character to another's speech may take the place on Television of an answering speech. It may indeed take the place of a whole walk round the stage before the delivery of the answering speech.

A certain amount of film is permissible in Television plays. Here again the demand should not be overdone. Six minutes of film is about the limit. A few feet of film cut into a play here and there open it up and give it spaciousness. An exorbitant amount of film overloads the play, besides costing money. An author should keep his filming out of doors, on location. He should also try to contrive it without dialogue. A sound-track may be added to it afterwards. But a demand for film picture and dialogue together presents difficulties, as a sound-truck is not always available.

IV

THE smallness of the Television screen prohibits the use of many characters in a Television play. Directors can do wonders. But Television is not at its best when trying to depict a herd of elephants, and a large number of actors gathered together on the screen is apt to look like a football group. There is no hard and fast limit to the size of a cast. An author would do well, however, to arrange his play in such a way that no more than two, three or four of his characters are on the screen at the same time. If he requires more, he must see to it that they appear in different scenes. The most effective scenes on Television are two-handers. And many scenes are played with a single character in vision or, alternatively, with a second character reacting to the off-screen speech of the first.

V

THAT is about all there is to be said about the layout of a Television play.

There are, however, one or two practical points I should like to make.

Television sets are erected simultaneously. They do not have to be struck as in the theatre. And the camera can move fairly easily from one to another. Not so the actor. He is far less mobile. If the author wishes him to go from set A to set B he must give him time to get there either by injecting film or by writing dialogue for other characters.

He must also give him time to change his clothes. In a film, an actor can finish one sequence in running shorts and appear, a second later, wearing tails. The Television actor is not capable of such sleight of hand. Time must be allowed him in the script, even though there may be a quick-change dressing-room on the set. Overquick changes fuss an actor and make him nervous. Nine times out of ten they are unnecessary and are due merely to slovenly construction on the part of the author.

The same is true of make-up. Very often in the theatre an interval enables an actor to disguise himself or to put on or take off years. On Television it is much more difficult. For one thing the camera is closer to the actor than is the audience in a theatre, and quickly shows up make-up deficiencies. An actor may get by in the theatre with a line or two of make-up and a little false hair. On Television he must have time to make a change that will be convincing even in close-up.

These, I hope, are commonsense points, and the author will save his director a lot of trouble if he makes a note of them.

VI

FINALLY, I hope that authors will not be discouraged from writing for Television by a feeling that they are ignorant of Television technique. It is a technique that can easily be learned. For there are plenty of good technicians but there are very few capable authors. In the ultimate analysis it is the play that counts. And the author is the only man who can write it. If it has faults, there will always be someone to put them right.

N.B.—The following elementary Television terms may be of value:

LONG SHOT (LS)	=	what it implies.
MID SHOT (MS)	=	from the waist up.
CLOSE UP (CU)	=	head and shoulders.
BIG HEAD	=	head alone.
TRACK	=	to move the camera on its dolly from one point to another while keeping it focused on the action.
PAN	=	to move the camera from one point to another while keeping it on a fixed base.
CUT	=	to cut directly from one picture to another.

MIX	=	to mix one picture into another.
FADE	=	to let the picture fade out.
DISSOLVE	=	to let the picture go out of focus and disintegrate.
GRAMS	=	recorded music.
BP	=	back projection.

Chapter V

Other Programmes

I

I HAVE written so far exclusively about the Television play. There are, of course, many other means by which an author can contribute to BBC Television programmes. All departments of the BBC are eager for ideas and synopses, and, when these are good, authors are encouraged to work on them. The basic layout, however, for all scripts is much the same, and what I have written about plays applies also, with modifications, to other forms of Television writing.

II

SERIALS

A SPECIAL place is reserved in BBC Television programmes for serials. These are normally presented in six weekly parts, each part running for half an hour. Sound Broadcasting uses many serialized novels. Television prefers originals, although serials from novels are also considered.

Technically, a Television serial is based on the old cliff-hanging formulas of silent films or, more remotely, on the Victorian novels which used to be published in weekly or monthly instalments. There is no standard pattern for serials, but experience shows that certain ingredients are essential. The most important of these is suspense. A serial which holds the viewers' attention and keeps them guessing at the end of each episode is half-way towards being a success. It is usual to have one or two main characters running through all six parts. These help to focus attention and bind the story together.

A serial does not need a great many sets—about five is normal—but these sets should be constantly rotated and the changes rung between them. The story can also be kept moving by the use of scraps of film and of small subsidiary sets, and no scene should play long enough to allow the viewers to get bored with it. Action in Television serials counts for more than psychology, and small invention is more valuable than deep characterization. Once the actors are established the viewers expect a great deal to happen to them. And, of course, each episode of a serial should end with an unresolved question.

A certain amount of recapitulation is necessary at the beginning of the second and third parts of a serial. After that the viewer, switching on in the middle, will have to take his chance. With luck the second half of a good serial will be more or less self-explanatory. In any case, although it is bound to be complicated, with plenty of false clues and red herrings, a serial should never become confusing.

Needless to say, no author should submit full scripts of serials. All the BBC requires of him, in the first instance, is a breakdown in detail of his story and a few pages of dialogue.

III

SERIES

A SERIES is quite another matter and requires an entirely different approach. A serial is a three-hour story divided into six consecutive episodes. A series, on the other hand, is a string of incidents, each complete in itself, the whole held together by a theme or by a single character or group of characters. Once the theme or personality is established a series can go on for ever and ever.

When planning a series for the BBC an author should do no more than suggest an idea or, if he feels up to it, submit a pilot script. Series are often built round actors, and, if the particular actor envisaged by the author is not available, it is possible that no other actor will be able to play the part.

With its single programme and shortage of studio space the BBC Television Service cannot embark very frequently on a series. In the United States, of course, where channels are two-a-penny, weekly and even daily series are a common feature of Television programmes and appear to be very popular. And it is probable that commercial Television, whoever controls what, will be badly in need of series. In advertising, after all, one of the basic principles is continuity. The American habit is to budget for series in blocks of a minimum of thirteen scripts, and an author undertaking such a commission must know a great deal about Television technique, and must be prepared to write full camera scripts, giving an accurate estimate of what they will cost to produce, what sets they will need and how much location filming will be required.

IV

ADAPTATIONS

OWING to the shortage of experienced Television writers, the BBC has been forced to fall back, for many of its dramatic programmes, on adaptations of work originally designed for other mediums.

Most adaptations in the past have been of stage plays,

which are more readily turned into Television plays than are other forms of writing. Whenever an author is available and willing, the BBC invites him to collaborate in the adaptation of his play. And in no case are adaptations made without the author's knowledge and consent. Some authors enjoy the opportunity of working on their own plays. Others, having grown tired of their subjects, are content to leave adaptation to the BBC Script Section or to individual directors. Dead authors, of course, have to take their chance.

The most difficult plays to adapt are comedies, which consist, roughly speaking, of dialogue, character and situation. The situation must stand and the characters can scarcely be cut. There remains only the dialogue, and, when comedy dialogue is cut, the chances are that the comedy will be cut with it. This is a constant problem. The only solution to it is that authors should write their comedies with Television presentation in mind.

The adaptation of stage plays, old and new, is normally undertaken by BBC staff writers and directors, and outside writers are rarely called in to adapt the work of their playwright colleagues. Most plays, after all, require no more than rigorous pruning, a little transposition of scenes and a general opening up. For these purposes it is not as a rule necessary and certainly not economic to commission outside writers.

Novels and stories are another matter. The English language abounds with brilliant stories, many of which are suitable for adaptation into Television terms. And here the outside author can find plenty of work.

He must remember, however, that, unless he proposes to adapt the work of an author who has been dead for fifty years or more, he will run up against copyright. Living authors and the estates of recently dead ones are at liberty to refuse permission for the adaptation of their work, and frequently do so. Before embarking on an adaptation, therefore, an author should check with the BBC to make sure that his subject is clear for copyright, that the BBC consider him a suitable adaptor and that another adaptation is not already in existence.

Turning a distinguished story or novel into a Television play is often a major creative and selective job.

I should perhaps warn would-be adaptors that some of our best story-tellers are most intractable. Take Dickens. At first glance he seems easy. He has such vitality, such movement, such power to hold the attention. On closer examination, he turns out to be very difficult, because so often his action is in his prose and not in his dialogue. It is no good thinking, for example, that a Television play can be made out of the *Pickwick Papers* merely by taking a pair of scissors and cutting out the dialogue. If an adaptor does that, he will find that he is left with a series of scenes in which various characters sit in various hostelries drinking brandy and hot water and discussing their adventures. The whole movement of the *Pickwick Papers* is in those fabulous coach journeys, in runaway horses, hats and coat-tails flying, objects and characters spinning through the air, in fact in the prose. If an adaptor wants to adapt the *Pickwick Papers* he must be confident that he can translate the prose of Dickens into Dickensian dialogue. And that is no easy task.

V

TRANSLATIONS

FINALLY, translations. The BBC Television Service produces many plays translated and adapted from foreign languages. And, as time goes on and Eurovision becomes a reality, it will no doubt produce many more. If he is qualified to do so, there is no reason at all why the outside author should not have a hand in these. He should realize, however, that most distinguished foreign authors have their own English translators. And it is usually inadvisable for a writer to translate a foreign play 'on spec'. Many authors do this only to find that the translation rights are tied up and that an official translation already exists. Before translating a foreign play an author should check with the BBC, as he does with English novels and stories, to make sure, first of all that the BBC is interested, and secondly that the rights are free.

So far as possible the BBC makes its own contacts direct with foreign authors or their agents and either commissions translations and adaptations to be made by outside authors or does the work itself.

Incidentally, the BBC can cope with most foreign languages and prefers to have a play in the original than tied, as is so often the case, to a bad translation. Indeed, the BBC has frequently been unable to produce a foreign play because its author had foolishly given the translation rights to an unworthy translator.

VI

OF the BBC Television Departments, the Drama Department is probably the largest employer of outside writing talent, closely followed by Children's Programmes, which require many dramatic stories, designed for special age-groups. The Documentary Department relies on its own producers to prepare a large proportion of its scripts. It does, however, employ a fair number of outside writers, mainly screenwriters, who are expected to know about scripting and also to do research. Although frequently written in dramatic form, documentary programmes are what their name implies. They are true life stories and must be absolutely accurate. The Music Department needs librettos. The Light Entertainment Department needs outside writers for its serials and, occasionally, for series. And both Talks and Light Entertainment are constantly on the look-out for programme material of all kinds. In addition, dramatized short stories are quite frequently presented by one department or another.

In short, there are many different channels of approach to the BBC Television Service. In all cases the author is advised to submit ideas and synopses rather than completed scripts. He is also advised to send his submissions to heads of departments, not to individual producers or directors. A director may be ill or on leave or busy on another programme. And, if a play is sent to him direct, he will invariably send it in to be read and criticized before taking action on it himself. So the author will save himself and everybody else both time and trouble if he submits his play through the correct channels. If he knows a director personally or admires his particular style of work, he can, of course, in a covering letter, ask that this director may be shown his play and asked to comment on it.

Chapter VI

Planning a Programme

I

AUTHORS complain sometimes that there is a delay between the submission of their work and its ultimate presentation on the Television screen. I can sympathize with their impatience. Nothing is more annoying than to have written a good play and then to have to sit around for month after month waiting to see it produced. Delays are, of course, inevitable in show business. Heaven knows, there are enough of them in the theatre. On Television, in addition to the normal delays caused by casting, costing and production, there is a further complication in that individual plays have to be fitted into a varied and flexible general programme.

It may perhaps be of help if I explain what happens to a script when it is sent to the BBC Television Service. Authors may then be able to realize just what hazards their work will have to encounter before it finally finds its place in a Television schedule.

II

EVERY week anything up to ninety scripts are submitted to the Television Drama Department alone. On top of that come programme ideas, and novels and stories which, it is suggested, might be suitable for adaptation. Ninety scripts is a lot of scripts, and, obviously, the majority of them are quite useless for transmission.

Nevertheless, the BBC being a public service, each one is acknowledged and read, and those that are not wanted are returned within two weeks. The rest are sifted and re-read. And the most promising are very carefully studied. A synopsis is made of them. They are classified for type and length, and an estimate is made of what they will cost to produce, how many sets they will require and what filming will be needed. Finally, a short list is compiled and, from this short list, the Head of Drama makes his selections for his quarterly programme.

It is here that the first delays occur. For a great many factors have to be taken into consideration before any one play can be sure of finding its correct place in the general schedule.

III

THE Drama Department has a dual function. On the one hand it has been for many years a repertory theatre. Week after week it presents to viewers Television versions of outstanding theatre plays by authors of all nationalities and all generations. On the other hand it has a growing and gladly undertaken responsibility for finding new work by new authors and giving it an airing.

So far, the balance between old and new has not been struck, for the simple reason that, although a great many scripts are submitted, very few are good enough to put serious pressure on established plays. The majority of scripts submitted are still in stage-play form. And authors would do well to remember that plays of this kind are in competition with all the masterpieces of the theatre. Occasionally, a first-class new stage play turns up. More often a great deal of work has to be done inside the BBC to bring a new stage play up to competitive level.

By this I do not mean that the BBC is not interested in new stage plays. But those authors who have taken the trouble to design their plays expressly for the Television medium are given priority.

In the United States, where the need for advertising plugs makes it virtually impossible to produce a play that runs for more than fifty-four minutes, the supply of stage plays which can be suitably gutted for Television purposes has just about dried up. In this country, however, where time-schedules are not controlled by advertisers, the BBC Television Service continues to present a high-standard, stage-play repertory programme. Sooner or later, of course, when more and more authors become proficient in Television technique, the BBC will have to put a limit to its stage play productions. But that time is not yet. Meanwhile, although the supply of stage plays is enormous, a big effort is being made to encourage authors to experiment with new ideas and new techniques. How big that effort is may be judged by a few figures.

In 1950, the BBC Television Drama Department produced 105 plays. Of these all except ten were Television adaptations of established theatre plays.

In 1954, on the other hand, out of a similar total, only 30 productions were of established theatre plays. The rest were either special adaptations of new plays, adaptations of stories and novels, or new plays written expressly for the medium.

In addition, the department produced four full-length serials, three of them entirely new, the fourth a special adaptation of a novel.

This encouragement of authors new to Television entails a great deal of work. Dead authors, after all, are far easier to handle than live ones. Dead authors did at least finish their plays before they died. Live authors, on the other hand, are subject to human frailty. A few are most professional about their delivery dates. Most of them, however, take longer than they had anticipated to finish their scripts, or fall ill, or get knocked down in the street, or take up appointments abroad, or are lured away into other and more lucrative engagements. Delays, in a word, are often caused by authors themselves. And the BBC has learned from bitter experience not to schedule plays until the scripts are completed.

IV

ONCE the Head of Drama has blended his programme to his own satisfaction, the old play with the new, comedy with tragedy, the generally popular with the intellectually more adventurous, the traditional with the experimental, he has to face greater vicissitudes than normally befall any theatrical manager.

First, he may run up against copyright. Film companies are constantly buying up the copyright of plays, and, as Television is still regarded by the cinema industry as a dangerous competitor, there is always a large number of plays which may be played in the West End, on tour, in provincial repertories, by amateurs and by Sound radio, but which are not available for production on Television.

Then there is the director problem. BBC directors are versatile, but are apt to have their own preferences and their own strengths. Thus, one director may work miracles with a standard play, whereas another is at his best only when challenged by a script requiring adventurous technical handling. Often a particular play may be held up until the director best suited to produce it is available.

A similar problem arises over casting. Many plays can be cast in a dozen different ways. But a few need special casting. And, although Television is not tied to star-casting to anything like the same extent as is the theatre, there are some plays which demand a dominant personality. And he or she may not always be available when required.

Finally, there is the general question of costing and sets. Certain plays may turn out to be too heavy for a quarter which is already expensive and may have to be postponed until the next. And the Design and Supply Department, which services all the producing departments, may find that it is already too deeply committed in scene-loads and man-hours to undertake another big production.

V

EVEN when the Head of Drama has solved his own internal scheduling problems he has still to face competition from other producing departments.

BBC Television programmes are planned about six months ahead. And it is rare indeed that any head of department finds himself with a free hand to carry out all his original plans.

There are eight producing departments in the Service: News, Films, Outside Broadcasts, Talks, Documentary, Children's Programmes, Light Entertainment and Drama. Each of these departments bids for time on the general programme, and this time is not allotted until the Controller of Programmes has considered the balance of the total offering and its cost.

The Head of Drama normally expects to have to provide a full-length play on Sunday night of sufficient interest to be worth repeating on the following Thursday, and a play on Tuesday night for a single performance. In addition, he must be prepared to provide serials and a number of plays of varying length for odd occasions.

These are his normal expectations. But anything can happen on Television. The Sunday night play, for example, may go out of the schedule because an opportunity has arisen to present an ice-show or a circus. The carefully-planned ninety-minute play for Tuesday may have to be replaced by one of sixty minutes because the second half of a concert has unexpectedly become available. Or a production may be held up until it becomes known whether or not the BBC will be allowed to broadcast the telerecording of a football match. Or a Eurovision relay may turn up. Or a Cabinet Minister may want to make a speech. Or the head of another department may find that his programmes look sombre and should be set off by something more light-hearted than was intended by Drama.

The strength of the BBC Television Service is its flexibility. But this same flexibility is bound to have repercussions on individual programmes. And the author may have to suffer, either because his play has had to be postponed, or because it is being held in reserve.

VI

THIS is a slightly depressing picture. And it is true that there are occasionally plays which, for one reason or another, seem to elude scheduling for a very long time. A more hopeful feature is that, in fact, in spite of all difficulties, over a hundred plays of varying length and of widely different types are produced every year by the Drama Department.

Any author who has had to do with show business will appreciate the need for patience. And the BBC has an advantage over most commercial managements in that it is unlikely to go abruptly out of business.

I need hardly add that, on the rare occasions when a really first-class play comes along, all difficulties seem to disappear, and the play shoulders its way into the schedule, as does any outstanding work in any medium.

Chapter VII

The Creation of a Script

I

I WANT now to show what can be the result of a successful collaboration between a Television director and an author.

I call him a director. Sometimes he calls himself a producer. It is all a little confusing. The ideal set-up is that of producer and director, in which the producer controls the production, pre-plans, discusses the script well in advance with the author, makes estimates of costing, etc., while the director takes rehearsals and directs the transmission in the studio. Unfortunately, such a set-up is rare. And the author will normally have to deal with only one man, whether he calls himself producer or director. To avoid confusion I shall refer to him as the director.

Most scripts reach the BBC in an advanced form, and only minor work is required on them. Let me assume for the moment that, for once in a while, we are able to start from scratch. An author has come into the Television Centre with his head full of ideas. He is a 'safe' author, and the BBC is prepared to commission him to write a play. A director has been appointed to work with him, and the Script Section is standing by to help and advise. I have shown already what problems an author usually has to face in his choice of subject and the relation of his particular play to the general programme. This time he is left in no doubt. The whole shape of the Drama schedule for the next six months is explained to him, and he is invited to provide a ninety-minute play worthy of two performances, and is given a dead-line. The director promises him all the time he can spare from his other productions. What happens next?

II

FIRST of all there are conferences, attended by the author, the director, the script supervisor and one of the script assistants. At these conferences the author's ideas are fully discussed. And there is a measure of disagreement. The BBC wants one thing. The author wants to do another. One play idea has already been covered in another programme. A second will be too expensive to realize. A third sounds too specialized. After a lot of argument it is eventually agreed that the author will write a play on, say, the great Quaker prison-reformer, Elizabeth Fry. She is a character who appeals to him, and he knows a good deal about her period. Incidentally this is a subject which the BBC Television Service has always wanted to tackle. A great many authors have had a shot at it. But so far no one has turned in anything worthy of production. This time we are more hopeful.

III

ELIZABETH FRY. What do we know about her? We put our heads together and find that we know quite a lot.

First, the bare bones. She was born in Norfolk, in 1780, of a prosperous and rather hilarious Quaker family. In 1800 she married a Quaker banker called Joseph Fry and had ten children. She died peacefully in the bosom of her family in 1845. So much for her domestic life. Her fame rests on her prison reform. She had always been interested in good works. One day, in London, in 1812, she was approached by an American Quaker, Stephen Grellet, who begged her to use her influence to improve the appalling conditions in which women prisoners were living in Newgate gaol. She accepted the challenge, went to the Governor, created order out of chaos, and went on from Newgate to make life pleasanter for all manner of unfortunate people, from lighthouse keepers who found themselves without literature, to convicts on their way to the penal settlements in Australia. She died full of honour and with an international reputation. An impressive life. But where is the play?

If we dig a little deeper, we find that there is plenty of drama. In her domestic life Elizabeth had to keep the peace between the Society of Friends and her beloved husband, who was very fond of music—a sin to the Quakers—and who was ultimately expelled from the Society when, through no fault of his own, he went bankrupt. And in her public life her work ran by no means smoothly. Although the Governor of Newgate became her ally, she was constantly being thwarted by officialdom in the person of the Home Secretary, Lord Sidmouth. There was conflict too in the rival claims of her family, of the Society of Friends and of her public duty.

IV

ALMOST of its own accord the pattern of a play emerges. The author, who has had much experience in the theatre, sees it first as a chronicle. His first act takes him through Elizabeth's early life and finishes with her marriage. His second act involves her with Newgate and rises to a crisis when her husband goes bankrupt and she is forced to retrench and to renounce her public work. His third act resolves her problems and leaves her dying, full of years and renown, and probably handing on her torch, in a touching death-bed scene, to Florence Nightingale. This may be all right for the theatre. But chronicles are no good for Television. For one thing, the passage of time presents too many problems. For another, even if it were possible to find an actress young enough to play the early scenes and mature enough to play the later ones, the costume and make-up changes would be almost impossible. Instead, the author is persuaded to set his scene in Elizabeth's middle years, taking up her story at the dramatic moment when she first meets Stephen Grellet, and setting it down as she watches the first orderly departure of a prison-ship for Australia. At this point the author remembers that he was once a screenwriter. He would dearly like to use the life of Mrs Fry as a thread on which to hang exciting pictures of Regency England: the streets of London, the Norfolk countryside, a Lord Mayor's banquet, the visit of Mrs Fry to Queen Charlotte. Here the director intervenes. The author must be sensible, he says. He must hold his play within the limits of what is possible on a Television screen. Reluctantly the author agrees.

V

WE now have a play in good historical shape. What about the flesh and blood? Comedy, for example. On the face of it Mrs Fry's life is a grim battle with adversity. Is there comedy to be had from it? Fortunately someone remembers that, in her youth, Mrs Fry was extremely gay. And, for all her beautiful poise and serenity, there was always laughter in her just below the surface. Comedy then with her childen. Comedy in her husband's skirmishes with the Plain Quakers. Comedy, perhaps, even in Newgate Gaol itself. Yes, the author does not feel that his play will be too sombre. And romance? This is more difficult. A devoted wife, living happily with her family, is certainly a noble sight but scarcely a subject for dramatic romance. The author will have to look elsewhere. To her children perhaps? Or why not a sub-plot involving a girl who falls in love with a thief? This idea pleases the author immensely. Certainly, he says. He will create a good girl who falls in love with a bad man, gets sentenced to death with him, and is finally reprieved and sent to Australia. This idea will kill two birds with one stone. It will lend romance to the story. Also, if he brings the girl early into Mrs Fry's life, he will be able to give her a personal motive for her interest in Newgate Gaol, for her intercession with the Home Secretary and, finally, for her efforts to improve the conditions of the poor wretches being shipped off to Australia.

VI

WHAT about sets? Here the director speaks up forcibly. The author really must be economical. If he spreads himself, the budget will get completely out of hand. And Design and Supply will not be able to cope. The author is not alarmed. He will need one main set, he says. It will be the sitting-room of Mrs Fry's London house, and, in it, will be shown the motivation for all the events of the first two-thirds of the play. He would like a country set—a garden set, perhaps? A BP slide?—for the end of the play. And what about Newgate? Here the director reassures him. He likes the idea of the plain Quaker dress set against the horrors of the prison with a splash of Regency colour intervening. He does not want to miss Newgate, and is prepared to shoot the Newgate scenes without any constructed sets at all. He also likes the final picture of Mrs Fry reading the Bible on a prison ship, with the convicts quietly listening, and sailors hanging from the rigging. That, he feels, should not be difficult to stage. After all, in 'Ninety Sail', King Charles reviews his fleet at Spithead from a simple rostrum, with BP plates of masts and sails in the background. This leaves the author with quite a lot of space in hand. He can have a corner of the Governor's office and another of Lord Sidmouth's room. He can have two or three more odd corners and perhaps a little film. If he constructs his play carefully and keeps his action moving, the settings for it should not be insuperably difficult.

VII

AND the cast? Well, the author will need time to think about this. He knows he must be prudent. But how can he do without his heroine, Mrs Fry? Or her husband, Joseph? Or her brother, Sam Gurney? Or at least two of her children? Or Stephen Grellet? Or some Quaker Elders? Or the Governor? Or Lord Sidmouth? Or his girl and her lover? Or servants and turnkeys? And, of course, there must be extras. He does not see how he can possibly ask for less than twenty characters. At this the director blenches and begins to talk about special budgets. But the author is not setting out to write a history of Regency England or of the Quaker movement. He is writing a play about Mrs Fry, her emotions, her difficulties, her achievement. He promises faithfully that he will not write a pageant. He will write as economically as he can, confining himself to as few characters as are consistent with the movement and the drama of his story.

And so he goes away. With him he takes a dossier on Mrs Fry, prepared by the BBC Research Department. He will read her inimitable diaries. He will read the admirable life of her by Janet Whitney. He will steep himself in biographies in order to get the flavour of the period. He will then abandon history and write a human story.

VIII

FROM time to time during the next few weeks he will ring up and ask for guidance on technical matters. When he has completed his breakdown he brings it in and discusses it with the Head of Drama, who approves it in principle and gives the director instructions to cost it and mark it down for the schedule.

The first treatment arrives and is tested and is probed by the script supervisor and the director. The designer goes into a long huddle with the director. Finally, the finished script is passed to the Script Secretariat to be duplicated.

And now the ball passes from the author to the director.

Chapter VIII

Production

I

A TELEVISION director is a busy person. He rarely has more than five weeks for a play. And the author will only be able to catch him at weekends, occasionally in the evening, or when he comes up for air between productions. During the incubating period of a script the author will have assigned to him a script assistant who knows the director's methods and can keep the author on the rails.

Not until the director has put his latest production on the air will he be able to give his full attention to the new script. By this time he will have discussed it with his designer, made a bid for film, and consulted Wardrobe about costumes, some of which will be hired and some made on the premises. If casting is likely to be difficult, he will also have made tentative inquiries through the Bookings Department about the availability of artists.

Some five weeks before transmission he will get down to the serious business of casting, sending off copies of the script to leading actors and actresses and holding auditions for the rest. In casting, the author's wishes are naturally considered, although a wise author will leave most of the casting to the director, who knows the habits of the various artists and how they look and behave in front of the cameras.

His casting settled, the director will prepare his

camera script. And here the author's scribbles in the left-hand column will be invaluable.

The director's first assignment, when his casting and camera-scripting are completed, will be to go out on location and do his exterior filming. Only then will he be ready to rehearse the play.

II

A BBC Television play is rehearsed for either two or three weeks according to its complexity. Most of the rehearsals take place in outside rehearsal rooms, and the cast spends only two days, including transmission day, in the Television studio.

Outside rehearsals are normally held in remote and inaccessible halls belonging to boys' clubs or similar organizations. The back rooms of pubs, so often hired for the rehearsal of theatre plays, are of no use to Television. The director usually needs far too much space. A Television studio, after all, is in size more like a modest film studio than a theatre. In time, the BBC will have its own rehearsal rooms at the Television Centre. Meanwhile, directors, staff and casts have to suffer—and travel.

I would not care to pontificate on the desirability of an author attending his own rehearsals. It depends on the author, on the director, and, of course, on the cast. The late Sir Arthur Pinero used to assemble his cast before a production and solemnly read his new play through to them. From that moment not a comma could be changed. Very few modern authors are in a position to take up such a dictatorial attitude. And very few, I think, would care to do so. The author must, however, be firm about his script. He should not allow it to go into rehearsal until both he and the director are happy about it, and, once it has been duplicated, only minor cuts and alterations should be considered. If the author once reveals that he has lost confidence in what he has written his cast will soon be at him like a pack of wolves, each with a number of helpful suggestions which, when added together, will completely alter the play. The author should always attend the first read-through of his script in order to clear up misunderstandings and to satisfy himself that the actors know what they are talking about. After that he should leave rehearsals to the director, occasionally watching a run-through, and being prepared to turn up quickly in an emergency. An author who attends every single rehearsal usually gets in the way. Also, he is likely to become confused. For a Television rehearsal is not at all like the rehearsal of a theatre play. There is no steady sweep to the footlights. Instead, the floor will be covered with peculiar chalk-marks, and the director will be forever huddling the actors together to make quite sure that, when they get into the studio, they will be properly grouped for the cameras. Very often he will be concerned merely with a profile or the back of a head. A Television rehearsal will not make sense to an author unless he constantly realizes that what he is watching is not a scene played through, but a series of embryo tiny pictures.

With him at rehearsal the director will have his secretary, who will keep an eye on the script and make exact notes of the camera changes he will require. By the time of transmission she will know as much about the script as he does. Also at rehearsal will be the stage-manager, who holds the book and takes care of the props, and the studio-manager, who will be a shadowy figure at first but will later be in charge of the floor of the studio.

During rehearsals there will be an early visit from Wardrobe. Measurements will be taken and, one by one, the various actors and actresses will slip away for a fitting with the costumier. During the later stages of rehearsal there will probably also be a visit from the chief cameraman and from the chief lighting engineer, who like to know in advance what is going to be expected of them on transmission.

III

FOR a Sunday play the production moves over into the studio on Saturday morning. Here for the first time the actors put on their costumes and the author sees his sets. They will probably appal him. While no doubt admiring their individual beauty and ingenuity he will be quite unable to understand how any pattern, any coherence even can possibly emerge from so many bits and pieces.

The first day in the studio is given over to the cameras, and actors walk through their parts, doing only enough acting to satisfy the cameras that they are in shot and the lighting engineers that they are properly lit.

The studio-manager, as I have said, is in charge of the floor of the studio. Wearing head-phones, he takes instructions from the director in the gallery.

For a major production there are probably four cameras. One of these, the Iron Man, which is barely mobile, is at first trained on the roller-captions and is later used mainly for close-ups. Each of the other cameras is manned by a cameraman, also wearing head-phones, who, even if his camera happens to be mechanized, has with him his winder and dolly-pusher. Boom-operators—a skilled job this—wield microphones on the end of what look like fishing-rods, moving them in such a way that they are in reach of the actors, but not, it is hoped, in sight of the cameras. Electrical engineers watch the lighting. And at the side of the studio are a crew in charge of BP plates and screens.

There is a stage-manager, possibly two. One of these holds the book and acts as prompter. Viewers may sometimes wonder why they never hear prompts. This is not because of any special infallibility on the part of actors when they are in a Television studio. On the contrary, Television, with its many distractions, does, in fact, dry up actors quite frequently. But the prompter, when he sees an actor falter, immediately presses a button which automatically takes the sound off the air. He then gives the actor his line. A skilled actor can take a prompt without letting the viewers realize that he has done so. Only when there is music over the dialogue or a sound-effect or when the studio happens to be unusually noisy is the sudden deadness of sound noticeable.

The population of a studio varies with the size of the production. There will certainly be property-men, stage-hands, the designer, a fireman, an on-call carpenter, dressers, make-up girls, a call boy, representatives of Wardrobe, possibly Press men and, unless the director is very strict, a bunch or two of visitors.

The author himself, whatever his instructions, will be sure to get in the way of somebody or other. He will fall over cables, walk in front of BP screens, whisper to actors just as they are about to make entrances, and show a well-meant but thwarting interest in camera-lenses and other technical devices. As I have said before, dead authors are really a great deal more accommodating than live ones. In studios, authors should always try to be as dead as possible.

IV

CONTROLLING all this activity in the studio is the director, who sits behind a large sheet of plate glass in the gallery. He can see the studio but does not look at it. His attention is concentrated on the monitor in front of him, which shows the picture as it will go out on transmission. Alongside his transmission monitor are the preview monitors, each one showing the picture as seen by one of the individual cameras. While keeping his eye on the main picture the director gives instructions to the other cameras on the floor, making quite sure that, when each one's turn comes, it will give him the picture he wants.

Beside him in the gallery sits his secretary, watching the script and warning him in advance of the coming changes in pictures, lighting and sound. With him also, are his TOM (Technical Operations Manager), his vision-mixer, who punches up the picture for him, and his grams-operator, who fades in and out his musical effects. If there are film-inserts, he 'cues Telecine', and the film appears, ready to be punched up along with the studio camera pictures.

Somewhere beneath the gallery, and hidden from view, sit the Racks boys, whose job it is to prepare each picture before it goes out on the air.

V

THE author will find camera-rehearsals disconcerting. Some scenes will be played through over and over again. Others will be virtually ignored. Not until Sunday afternoon is he likely to see a full run-through of his play. He should watch this, if possible, in the gallery with the director. It is here that he will be able to see the machine working and learn what lessons there are for him to learn. And here at last he will be able to understand what pictures the director had in mind when he went into those long, long huddles with his designer and with his camera-men.

For the actual transmission I should advise the author to tear himself away from the confusion of the studio and view his play either in the viewing-room or, better still, on his own set at home.

VI

NO author, however experienced, can watch his play going out on the air without emotion. It is his brain-child. He has contained it for months. And now it is being suddenly exposed to the critical eyes of millions of strangers. All through the transmission he is tense. Not until the credit-captions come rolling up and the music fades away does he dare to relax. And it is with something of a shock that he hears the announcer calmly packing his play away for the night. No comment on the production or on the performances. No hint at the quality of his writing. Just a matter-of-fact statement that viewers will be able to see the play again on Thursday. And then on to the next item in the evening's entertainment. The author forgets that this is only one play in many plays and that all the plays in the year are only a fractional part of the endless belt of Television programmes.

But the director has not forgotten. Unlike the author he has no time to ruminate on the goodness or badness of the transmission. Already he is tetchily asking his secretary how long he is going to have to wait for the scripts for his next production and whether Miss Blank is likely to be free.

Chapter IX

Money

AUTHORS have to live. Or so they say. And the biggest difficulty in getting them to write for Television is that the BBC has so rarely been able to pay them enough money.

I

WITH established theatre plays there is no problem. An established theatre play, when produced on Television, is assumed to have made its mark and its money already in the theatre. The BBC fee represents a kind of bonus to the author, and often gives an old play a new lease of life with the repertory and amateur companies.

For a single performance of a theatre play the BBC pays £1 a minute for the first ten minutes; 15s. a minute for the next eighty minutes; 10s. a minute for any further minutes; plus fifty per cent extra for a repeat.

A few very well-known authors get slightly more. And any author who chooses to make a Television adaptation of his own play is offered extra money to do so.

II

WITH untried theatre plays the situation is slightly different. Quite obviously the BBC can never pay for an untried theatre play fees which in any way compare with what the author can earn from a successful West

End run. I think that most authors realize this. Certainly the vast majority of theatre plays submitted to the BBC have already been the rounds of the managements and have been, for one reason or another, rejected. And I personally feel that any author who submitted a first-class theatre play to the BBC before trying it out on theatre managements would be very foolish.

The BBC Television Service is, however, an excellent try-out theatre. And it is on this basis that it should be considered. After all, there are very few money-making plays, but there are many potential money-makers which misfire owing to premature production in unfavourable circumstances. The advantages to an author in having his play tried out on Television are manifold.

First, he will get his play knocked into shape by experienced script-writers and directors.

Second, he will get better casting and production than a normal try-out theatre can afford.

Third, he will get his name known to millions of people.

Fourth, he will get his play seen by theatre managers, many of whom cannot or will not read, or, at least, cannot always tell good theatre material when they do read.

Fifth, he will get criticisms from all the newspapers.

Sixth, he will retain all the rights in his work. Having once produced an author's play, the BBC does not keep a percentage interest in it.

III

THE writing of material specially designed for the Television medium is a different matter altogether. For original ninety-minute plays, Television pays the same basic fees as Sound: £120 for a single performance and £60 for a repeat.

This means that an author can usually count on earning something under £200 for an original. This is not a negligible sum. But to an experienced writer it is not particularly inspiring. Indeed, whereas an author, if he strikes lucky, can make a fortune out of a play or a film or a novel, he can scarcely make a living out of Television, even if he writes ten plays a year and gets them all accepted.

Fortunately there are signs that first-class Television writers are beginning to be appreciated. And it is quite certain that they will be able to command, in the future, substantially higher fees than they have been able to obtain in the past.

I have spoken to many authors who feel that they cannot afford the time and energy required to learn the Television medium and write for it. I entirely understand their reluctance. There are, however, certain imponderables which should be taken into consideration. For example, Television is expanding at an enormous rate, not only in this country, but all over the world. There is already a dearth of scripts. In time that dearth will become acute. And undoubtedly a skilled Television writer will be able to command high fees. As an insurance policy against the future I think that all experienced authors should make time to have a shot at writing for Television, even if they jib at the money offered.

Also, there are the foreign markets. Every year these are increasing. A successfully produced BBC Television script has a certain cachet, and can earn royalties in many currencies. Moreover, although most foreign countries have by now developed their own Radio writers, very few of them have so far developed any

Television writers at all. Every quarter the BBC Television Script Section prepares a bulletin which contains a great deal of information about the Television plays the BBC has produced and proposes to produce. This bulletin is circulated by the BBC Television liaison officer to all European stations and also to Canada and the United States. It is eagerly studied, and already many scripts are being sent for. The BBC cannot, of course, send scripts to other Services without the author's consent. But it does pull off a number of extra copies of scripts each week, and these are sent all over the world if the author so desires.

V

I HAVE noticed that successful authors think and talk a great deal about money. Sometimes they give the impression that the practice of their craft is of less importance to them than the money it earns them. Artistically there is no doubt that the BBC can fulfil an author's hopes and desires. Financially, he may have to be patient. But I do not think it is too optimistic to say that, if he proves his skill with the BBC, he will soon also be satisfied with his financial rewards.

Chapter X

Conclusion

PEOPLE are inclined to be snobbish about Television Drama and to regard it as a slightly disreputable member of the theatrical family. This seems to me to be a wrong attitude. Certainly the theatre and the cinema are great and glorious institutions. But Television has its own positive contributions to make to the dramatic tradition.

I

I HAVE heard it said that Television is a menace to the theatre. This is foolish. Anyway, the theatre has faced many menaces in its time—from Oliver Cromwell to the talking picture—and has survived them all. Long before men could read or write they delighted to gather round the fire to watch an enacted story. And long after Television has removed from them the necessity of either reading or writing, the living actor will still retain his magic. If the theatre is make-believe, then Television is the shadow of make-believe. And, much though we may enjoy seeing an actor on the screen, we shall always prefer to see him in the flesh.

At the moment Television is doing a good job by the theatre. It is acting as a sort of trailer both for actors and for authors. It is bringing the theatre into millions of homes and showing plays to millions of viewers who have not so far been theatre-goers. Ibsen, for example, has usually been considered a school-book dramatist, a writer for the minority. Television has proved him a living man of the theatre with a story for everyone. This can only do good to the theatre.

Nor can it be said that Television empties the theatres. The standard of acting and production is sufficiently high on Television to harm bad Reps and little touring companies. But it has made no impression at all on the business of the West End, of the first-class touring companies or of the best of the local theatres. Indeed it has done them good. One play, for example, which was first produced on Television and then shown in the theatre, drew, for the months of its run, large numbers of people who had already seen it on Television.

In the future the theatre will, I believe, have a lot to learn from Television. The quality of acting in the English theatre is probably better today than anywhere else in the world. But, structurally, the English theatre has hardly progressed at all since the XVIIIth Century. Television has discarded footlights and the proscenium arch. And authors are no longer restricted to conventions that died with gas. In time the effects of this new freedom will be felt in the theatre. And theatres will be built to suit authors—as has been done at Stratford—instead of authors being forced, as they so far have been, to restrict themselves to existing theatre structures.

II

THE effect of Television on the cinema is slightly different. The cinema is big business. And big business is inclined to prosper through its bad products as well as through its good. Undoubtedly a fine film will always draw its audience. And Television cannot and should not compete. But whereas, for many years, families were wont to visit their local cinema twice a week whatever the picture showing, they now visit it only when there is a film which they positively want to see. On other nights they find it cheaper and more convenient to take a chance with their Television sets. And the standard of Television plays does not have to be terribly high to kill B pictures. In a word, Television is a menace to bad pictures and no sort of challenge at all to good ones.

III

ACTORS are, of course, of great importance to an author. He can indeed do very little without them. Fortunately most of our distinguished English actors are now familiar with Television. Although some of them are still worried by the cameras and by the lack of an audience, most of them have made a point of appearing in Television plays between engagements in order to familiarize themselves with the technique and at the same time to keep their faces in front of the public. They know too that theatre and film managements often cast from Television. There are as yet very few pure Television actors. These will come in time.

IV

THE BBC has had a long battle to perfect the technique of Television production. That battle is nearly won. And, for the future, technique can be forgotten or taken for granted. Anyway, viewers do not really worry about technique. They are by now accustomed to a high standard of production. And they notice any slackness or falling off. But they care far more for ideas than for the method by which they are expressed. I have said already that authors should not bother themselves too much about technicalities. They must know the groundwork. The rest they can leave to the actors and to the directors.

V

ALREADY the future of Television is taking shape. A Television play is expensive to produce. And costs are steadily rising. It is safe therefore to assume that, in the future, Television plays will become simpler and more economical, with fewer actors and less elaborate sets. These economies, as it happens, are also in line with the way in which the best Television writers are thinking.

Television, as it grows up, will shake itself free from the influences of the theatre and of the cinema. And I am quite sure that, in future, it will occupy itself more and more with what goes on in men's heads, with the follies, disasters, idiosyncrasies and emotions of mankind. It is an intimate medium and well suited to this task. It will not need the formal settings of the theatre. It will not need to emulate the pageantry of the cinema. Its job will be to lay bare what is in men's heads and hearts. In this job lies its true and great future.

NOTE

No one can learn to write a Television play—or anything else for that matter—just by reading a book. I have tried to compress into a few brief chapters all the information essential to an author who wishes to write for the BBC Television Service. But, obviously, practice is of more importance than theory. And I feel that the following quotations will be of more value to the would-be Television writer than anything I can tell him.

I am most grateful to the BBC for authorizing me to reproduce extracts from BBC copyright scripts. I am also grateful to the following authors for allowing me to quote from their work:
Caryl Doncaster, Iain MacCormick, Wolf Mankowitz, Donald Wilson, Michael Barry and Charles Terrot, to Carlotta Monterey O'Neill for the use of *The Emperor Jones*, to Secker and Warburg Ltd, for the use of *1984*, and to C. E. Webber, who wrote the radio script from the first episode in Henry Cecil's book *Ways and Means*.

QUOTATIONS FROM SCRIPTS

1. The Small Victory
2. Return to Living
3. The Emperor Jones
4. The Comedy of Errors
5. Shout Aloud Salvation
6. The Bespoke Overcoat
7. The Disagreeable Man
8. The Six Proud Walkers
9. '1984'
10. The Eye of a Gypsy

THE SMALL VICTORY

by *Iain MacCormick*

Produced by *Julian Amyes*

In 1954 Iain MacCormick wrote a cycle of four plays for Television. All four were complete in themselves, but each was bound to the other three by the same characters and by a continuing theme. I have quoted here the beginning of the third play. It is the script as the author submitted it, and before the producer had started to work on it. This play is true Television. The author wastes no time on background. He picks up his characters at a moment of crisis in their lives and plunges straight into his story.

FILM-ESTABLISHING SHOT—MISSION GATES—MLS—DAY

The mud-brick pillars are almost intact, except for the top of one, which is missing, blown somewhere by the blast of a shell . . . but the gates, between, lean drunkenly to one side, as if they had been pushed there by a heavy body anxious to make a way for itself. . . .

The scene is desolation. . . .

Two ragged, tiny children, hand in hand, come timidly past the CAMERA and into the scene. They pause for a moment as if afraid to go on, then slowly advance to the gate itself where they stand, peering inside to the courtyard that we cannot see . . . the little boy peeps around the corner of the pillar . . . there is nothing for him there . . . they go right up to the gate where, in the centre of it, is a plaque. . . .

We go into a close-up of the plaque which reads merely:

KOREAN MISSION OF THE SACRED HEART
FOR CHILDREN

Now, back in Medium Long Shot, we see the little boy reach up, touch the plaque with his fingers . . . he rubs a little dust from it which he later wipes-off on his clothing . . . then, hand-in-hand, the two children slowly turn away and, together, move out of sight . . . we have not seen their faces. . . .

TITLES

. . . As the titles fade we begin slowly to TRACK IN towards the gates and DISSOLVE TO

FULL SHOT OF CLASSROOM—MORNING

Now we are in a small classroom in this old, battered building and, although the room is not very well lighted, we can see all around us the evidence of children . . . some flowers are in a cup of water on what has been the teacher's desk . . . books lie open upon the forms . . . not books of great culture or learning, but simple books with pictures of fairies and flowers and ships and 'The Lord is my Shepherd' . . . and on the blackboard are more pictures of simple, elemental things and some Korean words chalked at the side of each . . . then, to the right of the blackboard has been built a tiny alcove, surmounted by a cross . . . the Crucifixion . . . and on the left, in a similar place, hangs a small, wooden Madonna. . . .

In one corner is a tilted heating stove with the great flue running back across the room . . . one piece of it hangs down, gaping, shaken there by a blast . . . some of the windows are broken, too and, in one, a length of hair-ribbon flutters in the draught, caught there by some freak of blast-wind.

As the camera wanders quietly through this room, we become aware of a door that is open and which leads to a small ante-room beyond . . . and another door which leads from that to the stair-head. . . .

The ante-room is obviously the teacher's room and a place for meditation . . . it is very barely furnished—only a table and two chairs . . . and a crucifix on the wall by the single narrow window. . . .

At the far end of the classroom is another door which gives directly on to the landing . . . this, too, is open.

As we have moved around we have become aware of one more presence, that of a priest, wearing the dark robes of his Mission . . . he is kneeling before the crucifix in the ante-room, we know that he is praying. . . .

Through the end door, into the classroom, comes the sturdy figure of a Nun, dressed in the white robe of her order . . . she pauses and looks around for someone, this chunky, middle-aged Swiss woman, SISTER ANNELISE. . . . She calls softly. . . .

ANNELISE: Father. . . . Father Riley. . . . .

The kneeling figure does not stir. SISTER ANNELISE moves slowly into the room where, almost at once, she sees the kneeling figure. . . . At once, she makes obeisance . . . the PADRE lifts his head, crosses himself and replies.

PADRE: (*Quietly*) Yes, Sister Annelise?

The NUN crosses herself and moves towards him, still slowly, without any emotion but a desire not to disturb him. . . .

ANNELISE: (*Softly*) Father—they have come.

PADRE: Oh.

He rises and we see him now for what he is . . . an ordinary man, American, in his late forties, balding a little, tiring a little, stiffening a little. . . . He makes his obeisance, turns and comes towards the Nun.

PADRE: How many are there?

ANNELISE: (*A shrug*) Twenty . . . thirty. . . .

PADRE: Any officers?

ANNELISE: Three. . . .

She counts them off on her fingers.

ANNELISE: A Colonel in a car. He had a Captain with him. A young officer marched with the men. . . .

PADRE: What are they?

ANNELISE: The Colonel is Chinese.

PADRE: Oh.

ANNELISE: The two Koreans, the Captain and the young one, speak English . . . the Captain very good.

PADRE: (*A slight smile*) 'Very well'—not 'Very good', Sister Annelise. One does something 'very well', not 'very good'.

ANNELISE: (*A twinkle*) If I did not sometimes make (the) mistakes you would have nothing to complain to me about. A man needs to complain—or—

PADRE: —'So we say in Switzerland.'

They both chuckle. It is obvious that these two respect and like each other, as friends should.

PADRE: (*Suddenly serious*) I had better go down and meet these people.

ANNELISE: There is no need. Father Robert is with them.

PADRE: Good.

He goes to the window and looks out.

ANNELISE: You won't see them from there. . . . They are all in the front.

PADRE: I was looking for the children. . . . I had forgotten.

PADRE: The fires are not so bright. Perhaps they have them under control now. . . .

He turns to ANNELISE.

PADRE: Will they allow us to bring the children back here?

ANNELISE: I don't know.

PADRE: We can't leave them out in the fields forever . . . four hundred children . . . even if they are safer out there.

ANNELISE: They will be safe enough here, now. There is no more firing in the City.

PADRE: How are we off for food?

ANNELISE: We have enough. The rice-bins are full and we have meat enough for a week—flour for three weeks. We have enough.

He peers out of the window again.

PADRE: How do 'they' seem?

ANNELISE: Who can tell? The young officer is all right, I think. But, the other two—who can tell?

PADRE: Why did they come here?

ANNELISE: (*Gently*) They have come—specially.

PADRE turns slowly to her.

PADRE: Specially?

ANNELISE: So Father Robert said. He said they came because they were sent by the General and the new Governor of the City.

PADRE: Sent for what?

ANNELISE: Father Robert did not know.

PADRE: I think I'd better go down and find out.

He moves towards the door, As he does, AN OFFICER appears in the doorway; he carries a revolver, loosely, in one hand. He is 28, a half-caste Korean—and his name is CAPTAIN FENG. When he speaks, he speaks quietly, almost without accent, except that of the cultured Englishman. He makes a half-bow.

FENG: Captain Feng. . . .

PADRE: Good morning, Captain.

FENG: You are Father Riley?

PADRE: That's right.

FENG: (*A nod*) I have already seen the Nun.

PADRE looks surprisingly at FENG. FENG smiles slightly.

FENG: They all look surprised—just like you. They all wonder why my English is so good—just like you. It is not new.

PADRE: Your English is—English.

FENG: So it should be. For seven years I attended an English School. . . .

He grows colder

FENG: (*Cold*) Seven years is long enough to learn.

He gestures to the classroom.

FENG: You teach them English here, too? Or should I say—American?

PADRE: A little. . . .
FENG: And what else besides?
PADRE: The three R's.
FENG: Also in English?
PADRE: Those that have an aptitude—yes. Mostly, they are taught Chinese.
FENG: By you?
PADRE: (*A slight smile*) I couldn't teach anyone Chinese.
FENG: Then who teaches them?
PADRE: Two of our younger priests—who are Chinese—and three lay-teachers—who are Korean.
FENG: Converts?
PADRE: Converts.

FENG moves around the room, looking at it.

FENG: (*Abruptly*) And about God, Jesus Christ and what-not?
PADRE: (*Evenly*) And what-not.

FENG, nettled, swings around upon him, as if he were about to say something rude . . . instead, he controls himself—and picks up a book, which he leafs through. . . .

FENG: I remember this. . . . I had it, too, when I was a child. . . . 'Tales from Alice in Wonderland' . . . very funny.

He does not look up, but continues leafing through the book.

FENG: What do you expect from us?
PADRE: (*Wryly*) I wish I knew.

RETURN TO LIVING

written and produced by

Caryl Doncaster

Caryl Doncaster is one of those rare people who can write and direct their own stories. The following brief extracts are from one of her successful Documentaries. The first extract is a scene as she wrote it. The second is the same scene when she had visualized it for the cameras.

(i)

	MRS FELLOWES: I'm grateful, Dad.
	MR MASON: I don't want gratitude, Joan. I did what any father would have done. You're living with me now—and I'll see you and the kid all right.But I won't have him anywhere near the place. I wouldn't give him stable room—and that's flat. You made a promise. Now's the time to stick by it.
MR MASON exits to the shop.	
MRS FELLOWES sits down in one of the chairs by the table. JOAN, a girl of ten, comes rushing in, ready for school.	
	JOAN: Bye Mum.
	MRS FELLOWES: Have you got a hankie?
	JOAN: Yes.
	MRS FELLOWES: Have you got your gloves?
	JOAN: Yes—one's got a hole in the finger.
	MRS FELLOWES: Well, put them on

and give me them to mend tonight. And don't forget to kiss Grandad before you go.

The bell on the shop door rings.

Noises off: Sound of raised voices from the shop.

JOAN: OK.

They both look up.

MRS FELLOWES looks up.

JIM arrives in the doorway, followed by MR MASON.

MRS FELLOWES puts her hand on JOAN'S shoulder.

JIM: (*very angry*) Well, what a welcome! Where's the champagne? Remember me? I'm the man you married. Or has that slipped your mind?

MR MASON: (*equally angry*) Don't answer him, Joan. (*To* JIM) If you don't leave this house at once, I'll 'phone the police.

JIM: Go ahead. 'Phone the police.

MRS FELLOWES: Dad, don't.

MR MASON: This is my house. Either he leaves or I phone the police.

JIM: You're asking for something to phone the police about. . . .

JOAN cowers behind her mother. She starts to cry.

MRS FELLOWES: (*To* JOAN) Run upstairs for a moment, Joan.

JIM: Leave her be. I'm entitled to have a look at my own daughter aren't I? Or is there a law? Come here and kiss your dad.

JOAN: Go away—oh go away.

MR MASON: If you don't go. . . .

JIM: So you've turned the child against me, too, have you?

MR MASON: If you don't go. . . .

MRS FELLOWES: *(re-asserting herself)* Listen to me, Jim. Nobody's turned the child away from you but yourself. She hasn't seen her father for three years.

JIM: It hasn't been a piece of cake where I've been, you know.

MRS FELLOWES: There you go—the same old Jim. Self, self, self. Have you ever thought that it hasn't been a piece of cake for us, either?

(ii)

MRS FELLOWES: I'm grateful, Dad.

CUE JOAN

MR MASON: I don't want gratitude, Joan. I did what any father would have done. You're living with me now—and I'll see you and the kid all right.But I won't have him anywhere near the place. I wouldn't give him stable room—and that's flat. You made a promise. Now's the time to stick by it.

PAN him to door.

102.
CUT TO CAM 3 (D2-24)
MS MRS FELLOWES.
PAN her to table.
HOLD JOAN as she comes in from stairs.

JOAN: Bye Mum.

As JOAN joins MRS FELLOWES.

MRS FELLOWES: Have you got a hankie?

103.
CUT TO CAM 4 (D3-24)
X-2-shot on JOAN.

JOAN: Yes.

MRS FELLOWES in L.f/g.
(Cam 3 change to 8)

MRS FELLOWES: Have you got your gloves?

104.
CUT TO CAM 1 (D5-24)
Med 2-shot JOAN and MRS FELLOWES.

JOAN: Yes—one's got a hole in the finger.

CUE VOICES
(Cam 4 to 16)

MRS FELLOWES: Well, put them on and I'll mend them tonight. And don't forget to kiss Grandad before you go.

CUE JIM

As they turn:

Noises off: Sound of raised voices from the shop.

105.
CUT TO CAM 4 (D3-16)
MS door.
JIM enters.

JOAN: OK.

106.
CUT TO CAM 3 (D2-8)
CU MRS FELLOWES.

JIM: Well, what a welcome!

107.
CUT TO CAM 4 (D3-16)
MS JIM at door.

Where's the champagne?

108.
CUT TO CAM 1 (D5-24)
2-shot MRS FELLOWES and JOAN.

Remember me?
I'm the man you married
—or has that slipped your mind?

MR MASON: (*equally angry*) Don't answer him, Joan.

109.
CUT TO CAM 4 (D3-16)
2-shot MASON and JIM.
(Cam 3 change to 16)

(*To JIM*) If you don't leave this house at once, I'l 'phone the police.

JIM: Go ahead. 'Phone the police.

MRS FELLOWES: Dad, don't.

MR MASON: This is my house. Either he leaves or I phone the police.

110.
CUT TO CAM 1 (D5-24)
2-shot JOAN and MRS FELLOWES.
TRACK BK as JIM comes in CAM R.

JIM: You're asking for something to phone the police about. . . .

MRS FELLOWES: (*To JOAN*) Run upstairs for a moment, Joan.

JIM: Leave her be. I'm entitled to have a look at my own daughter aren't I? Or is there a law? Come here and kiss your dad.

As JIM turns:

JOAN: Go away—oh go away.

111.
CUT TO CAM 3 (D2-16)
X-2-shot on JIM.
MR MASON in R.f/g.

MR MASON: If you don't go. . . .

JIM: So you've turned the child against me, too, have you?

	MR MASON: If you don't go. . . .
As JIM turns: 112. CUT TO CAM 4 (D3-16) X-2-shot on JIM. MRS FELLOWES in L.f/g.	MRS FELLOWES: *(re-asserting herself)* Listen to me, Jim. Nobody's turned the child away from you but yourself. She hasn't seen her father for three years.
(Cam 3 change to 24)	JIM: It hasn't been a piece of cake where I've been, you know.
	MRS FELLOWES: There you go—the same old Jim. Self, self, self. Have you ever thought that it hasn't been a piece of cake for us, either?
As she turns to JOAN: 113. CUT TO CAM 3 (D2-24) MLS Group. HOLD JIM in R.f/g.	

THE EMPEROR JONES

by *Eugene O'Neill*

Produced by *Alvin Rakoff*

The following quotation is from the end of the first play produced for Television by the young Canadian director, Alvin Rakoff. It is a straightforward and famous theatre play. My quotation shows how Alvin Rakoff envisaged it for the cameras.

He motions JONES *to stand on the stump—the auction block.* JONES *looks up, sees the figures on all sides, looks wildly for some opening to escape, sees none, screams and leaps*

to

get as far away from them as possible. He stands there, cowering, paralysed with horror. The Auctioneer begins his silent speech. He points to JONES*, appeals to the planters to see for themselves. Here is a good field hand, sound in wind and limb as they can see. Very strong still in spite of his being middle-aged. Look at that back. Look at those shoulders. Look at the muscles in his arms and his sturdy legs. Capable of any amount of hard labour. Moreover of a good disposition, intelligent and tractable. Will any gentleman start the bidding? The planters raise their fingers, make their bids. They are apparently all eager to possess* JONES*. The bidding is lively, the* *crowd interested. While this has been going on,* JONES *has been seized by the courage of desperation. He dares to look down and around him. Over his face abject terror gives way to mystification, to gradual realization—stutteringly:*

76.
CUT TO CAM 3 (8)
BCU

JONES: (*cont*) What you all doin', white folks? What's all dis? What you all lookin' at me fo'? What you doin' wid me, anyhow?

77.
CUT TO CAM 1 (24)
High angle.

(*Suddenly convulsed with raging hatred and fear*) Is dis a auction? Is you sellin' me like dey uster befo' the war? (*Jerking out his revolver just as the Auctioneer knocks him down to one of the planters—glaring from him to the purchaser*) And you sells me? And you buys me? I shows you I'se a free nigger, damn yo' souls!

78.
CUT TO CAM 3 (8)
After first gun shot.
Percussion faster.

(*He fires at the Auctioneer and at the planter with such rapidity that the two shots are almost simultaneous. Only blackness remains and silence broken by* JONES *as he rushes off, crying with fear—and by the quickened, ever louder beat of the tom-tom*)

79.
CUT TO CAM 1 (24)
As JONES turns.

FADE CAM 1

80.
FADE UP CAM 2 (16)

(JONES *in forest, his trousers have been so torn away that what is left of them is no better than a loin cloth. He flings himself full length, face downward on the ground, panting with exhaustion.*

JONES: (*cont*) Oh, Lawd, what I gwine do now? Ain't got no bullet left on'y de silver one. If mo' o' dem ha'nts come after me, how I gwine skeer dem away? Oh, Lawd, on'y de silver one left—an' I gotta save dat fo' luck. If I shoots dat one I'm a goner sho'! Lawd, it's black heah!

GRAMS:

81.

CUT TO CAM 1 (24)

Whar's de moon? Oh, Lawd, don't dis night evah come to an end?

GRAMS:

FLICKER

82.

(*By the sounds, he is feeling his way cautiously forward*) Dere! Dis feels like a clear space. I gotta lie down an' rest. I don't care if dem niggers does cotch me. I gotta rest, I gotta rest.

SUPERIMPOSE CAM 3

(*A row of seated figures can be seen behind* JONES. *They are sitting in crumpled, despairing attitudes, hunched, facing one another with their backs touching the forest walls as if they were shackled to them. All are negroes naked save for their loin cloths. At first they are silent and motionless. Then they begin to sway slowly forward towards each and back again in unison, as if they were laxly letting themselves follow the long roll of a ship at sea. At the same time a low melancholy murmur rises among them, increasing gradually by rhythmic degrees which seem to be directed and controlled by the throb of the tom-tom in the distance, to a long, tremulous wail of despair that reaches a certain pitch, unbearably acute, then falls by slow gradations of tone into silence and is taken up again.*

JONES *starts, looks up, sees the figures, and throws himself down again to shut out the sight.*

FADE OUT CAM 3

JONES turns.

A shudder of terror shakes his whole body as the wail rises up about him again. But the next time his voice, as if under some uncanny compulsion, starts with the others. As their chorus lifts he rises to a sitting posture similar to the others, swaying back and forth. His voice reaches the highest pitch of sorrow, of desolation)

Percussion faster as JONES breaks down.

FADE OUT CAM 1

83.

FADE UP CAM 2

On JONES running.

84.

CUT TO CAM 1 (24)

JONES on knees.

JONES: (*cont*) What—what is I doin'? What is—dis place? Seems like—seems like I know dat tree—an' dem stones—an' de river. I remember—seems like I been heah befo'. (*Tremblingly*) Oh, Gorry, I'se skeered in dis place! I'se skeered! Oh, Lawd, pertect dis sinner!

GRAMS: FLICKER

(*Crawling away from the altar, he cowers close to the ground, his face hidden, his shoulders heaving with sobs of hysterical fright*)

Percussion group sings.

85. CUT TO CAM 2 (24) As dancer turns. CAM 3 MOVE TO POSITION FOR LAST SCENE	*(The Witch-Doctor. The tree, as if he had sprung out of it, the figure of the Congo Witch-Doctor appears. He is wizened and old, naked except for the fur of some small animal tied about his waist, its bushy tail hanging down in front. His body is stained all over a bright red. Antelope horns are on each side of his head, branching upward. In one hand he carries a bone rattle, in the other a charm stick with a bunch of white cockatoo feathers tied to the end. A great number of glass beads and bone ornaments are about his neck, ears, wrists and ankles. He struts noiselessly with a queer prancing step to a position between* JONES *and the altar.*
86. CUT TO CAM 1 (24) 87. CUT TO CAM 2 *(As before)* On dancer. 88. CUT TO CAM 1 (24) BCU 89. CUT TO CAM 2 *(Switches)* On dancer.	*Then with a preliminary summoning stamp of his foot on the earth, he begins to dance and to chant. As if in response to his summons the beating of the tom-tom grows to a fierce, exultant boom whose throbs seem to fill the air with vibrating rhythm.* JONES *looks up, starts to spring to his feet, reaches a half-kneeling, half-squatting position and remains rigidly fixed there, paralysed with awed fascination by this new apparition. The Witch-Doctor sways, stamping with his foot, his bone rattle clicking the time. His voice rises and falls in a weird, monotonous*

90.
CUT TO CAM 1 (38)
CU eyes.

91.
CUT TO CAM 2 (24)
On dancer as before.

92.
CUT TO CAM 1 (24)
(On dancer's leap)

croon, without articulate word divisions. Gradually his dance becomes clearly one of a narrative in pantomime, his croon is an incantation, a charm to allay the fierceness of some implacable deity demanding sacrifice. He flees, he is pursued by devils, he hides, he flees again. Ever wilder and wilder becomes his flight, nearer and nearer draws the pursuing evil, more and more the spirit of terror gains possession of him. His croon, rising to intensity, is punctuated by shrill cries. JONES *has become completely hypnotized. His voice joins in the incantation, in the cries, he beats time with his hands and sways his body to and fro from the waist. The whole spirit and meaning of the dance has entered into him, has become his spirit. Finally, the theme of the pantomime halts on a howl of despair, and is taken up again in a note of savage hope. There is a salvation. The forces of evil demand sacrifice. They must be appeased.* JONES *seems to sense the meaning of this. It is he who must offer himself for sacrifice. He beats his forehead abjectly to the ground, moaning hysterically)*

93.
CUT TO CAM 2 (24)

JONES: (*cont*) Mercy, oh Lawd! Mercy! Mercy on dis po' sinner.

(*The Witch-Doctor springs to the river bank. He stretches out his arms and calls to some god within its depths. Then he*

	starts backward slowly, his arms remaining out. JONES *squirms on his belly nearer and nearer, moaning continually)*
Percussion faster after dancer kisses knife.	
94. CUT TO CAM 1 (24) *(After dancer kisses knife)*	JONES: Mercy, Lawd! Mercy!
95. CUT TO CAM 2 (24)	*(The Witch-Doctor's voice shrills out in furious exultation, the tom-tom beats madly.* JONES *cries out in a fierce, exhausted spasm of anguished pleading)*
96. CUT TO CAM 1 (24) *(After false stab)* Track back to show knife. CAM 2 MOVES TO OTHER SET	Lawd, save me! Lawd Jesus, heah my prayer! *(Immediately in answer to his prayer comes the thought of the one bullet left him. He snatches at his hip, shouting defiantly)*
Percussion faster? Singing stops at the shot.	De silver bullet! You don't git me yit! *(He fires.)*
FADE OUT CAM 1 CAM 1 MOVES TO OTHER POSITION FOR LAST SCENE	

WILLIAM SHAKESPEARE'S

THE COMEDY OF ERRORS

Adapted for Television by

Lionel Harris and *Robert McNab*

Music by *Julian Slade*

Produced by *Lionel Harris*

I quote here from the ingenious camera-script made by Lionel Harris for a musical version of 'The Comedy of Errors'. Of special interest is the use of mirrors for the two Dromios. This enabled both parts to be played by the same actor.

GROUP go.

HOLD SYRACUSE AND LUCIANA

148. CAM 2 Single EPHESUS.	DROMIO S: Master, shall I fetch your stuff from shipboard? ANTIPHOLUS E: Dromio, what stuff of mine hast thou embark'd?
149. CAM 4 *(As before)*	DROMIO S: Your goods that lay at host, sir, in the Centaur.
150. CAM 1 Group shot favouring SYRACUSE.	ANTIPHOLUS S: He speaks to me. I am your master, Dromio: Come, go with us, we'll look to that anon; Embrace thy brother there, rejoice with him.
151. CAM 4 Single DROMIO.	DROMIO S: There is a fat friend at your master's house, That kitchen'd me for you today at dinner: She now shall be my sister, not my wife.

G

152. CAM 2 Single DROMIO.	DROMIO E: Methinks you are my glass, and not my brother;
153. CAM 4 *(As before)*	I see by you I am a sweet-fac'd youth.
154. CAM 2 *(As before)*	Will you walk in to see their gossiping?
155. CAM 4 *(As before)*	DROMIO S: Not I, sir, you are my elder.
156. CAM 2 *(As before)*	DROMIO E: That's a question, how shall we try it?
157. CAM 4 *(As before)*	DROMIO S: We'll draw cuts for the senior, till then lead thou first.
158. CAM 2 *(As before)*	DROMIO E: Nay, then, thus: We came into the world like brother and brother;
159. CAM 1 Group shot favouring ABBESS. *(CAM 4 to Porcupine Set for Mirror superimposition shot.)*	And now let's go hand in hand, not one before another. ABBESS: Renowned Duke, vouchsafe to take the pains To go with us into the abbey here, And here at large discourse all our fortunes, And all that are assembled in this place, That by this sympathized one day's error Have suffered wrong: go, keep us company, And we shall make full satisfaction. The Duke, my husband, and my

children both,
And you the calendars of their nativity,
Come to a gossips' feast, and go with me;
After so long grief, such nativity!

DUKE:
With all my heart, I'll gossip at this feast.

(MUSIC)
DUET:
HOLD EPHESUS and ADRIANA
160.

'LET'S GO HAND IN HAND'
Let's go hand in hand, fond lover,
Side by side with one another,
Let's go hand in hand, fond lover,
Side by side and hand in hand.

Let's go hand in hand, fond lover,
Side by side with one another,
Let's go hand in hand, fond lover,
Side by side and hand in hand.

CAM 3
and
CAM 4
on DROMIO.
Mirror shot
and
Superimposing
Double image.

DROMIO S AND E:
We came into the world like brother and brother,
Now let's go in, not one before another,
We came into the world like brother and brother,
Now let's go hand in hand.

Hand in hand, in hand, in hand,
Let's go hand in hand, my brother,
Side by side with one another,
Let's go hand in hand, my brother,
Side by side, and hand in hand.

(PV.1. On Crowd for Dance round Square.)
161.
CAM 1
On CROWD for Dance round Square.

MUSIC FOR 'QUOTH'
(Not Sung)
Tis dinner-time, quoth I,
Quoth who,
Quoth I,

Your meat doth burn,
Quoth I,
My gold, quoth he.
The pig, quoth I, is burned,
Quoth I.
The pig is burn'd—mayhap the stye.
Quoth he
My gold,
Quoth who?
Quoth he,
Quoth I
The pig, quoth I, is burn'd, quoth I,
The pig is burn'd, mayhap the stye.
Quoth he.
My gold,
Quoth who?
Quoth he.
Quoth I.

'I SHALL NO MORE'
(*Sung*)
I shall no more, I shall no more.
I shall no more, no more, to sea, to sea,
Here shall I die, here shall I die,
Here shall I die, I die, ashore, ashore.

MUSIC FOR DANCE:
'HAND IN HAND'
(*Not Sung*)

162.	
ROLLER CAPTION:	Hand, in hand, in hand, in hand,
THE END	Let's go hand in hand, fond lover.
CAST:	Side by side with one another,
ending	Let's go hand in hand, fond lover.
Produced by Lionel Harris	Side by side, and hand in hand.
FADE OUT VISION	*FADE OUT SOUND*

SHOUT ALOUD SALVATION

by

Michael Barry and *Charles Terrot*

Produced by *Michael Barry*

'Shout Aloud Salvation' was something of a landmark in Television history. It was one of the very earliest attempts to write a full-scale play specially for the medium.

Preview:
Telecine: (Map)
CAM 2 (CU MISERABLE)
CAM 3 (On door)
CAM 1 (On stairs)
CAM 4 (LS on crowd)
CAM 5

VISION	SOUND
FADE UP TELECINE.	Disc: BD106
Shot 1: An outline map encloses a plain grey Britain against a darker background. The title, SHOUT ALOUD SALVATION, grows from the centre of this until the words fill the screen.	*Trumpets; approaching and crescendo, strident, compelling.*
Quick fade out title, and start to track in on Map. As camera moves, the Map is illuminated so that it glows and vibrates with light.	SHARP FADE OUT ON CLIMAX OF TRUMPETS. F/U CONTRASTING QUIET PASSAGE. *Music: Andante Cantabile.* LX1257 *AND HOLD UNDER:*
DISSOLVE (5')	WOMAN'S VOICE: (*recorded, close, piano con grazia*)
Shot 2: CU a Debutante, full Court dress (*circa* 1882)	The nineteenth century is three-quarters gone;

just completing downward movement of curtsey.	Smoothly the rich years pass—on rolling wheels; Tandem, carriage, hackney, brougham!
DISSOLVE (3′)	Beneath the trees, the landaus pause to watch A marquetry of dappled shadow frame
Shot 3: CU, the sharply defined shadow of the bust of Queen Victoria.	The fountain playing in the sun. Quick voices by the flower-beds chat and call, And music drifts across the skirt-swept lawn: A fair land on a summer afternoon? Eighteen hundred and . . . (*Fade away from Mic.*) MAN'S VOICE: Factory, mill-shed, mine and foundry! Pistons thrusting, swift impelling
SLOW MIX CAM 2 (Studio A) Ext. Station. Night. Big CU of first MISERABLE.	Oil-wet shafts of steel compelling Men to towns, and desolation In the dark Satanic slum, From whose depths the spirits squalor Cries to God its tale of dolour.

The miserable is a creature of the slums of the last century. Probably conceived and born in intoxication. The face is a dehumanized grey mass. The flesh hangs in folds. The eyes are glazed discs, so vacant as to be almost opaque. The body is a shapeless bundle of stinking rags.

TRACK back. A woman's slim and white hand enters the frame and rests upon the creature's shoulder. TRACK back to MS.	CROSSFADE MACHINE RHYTHM TO: GRAMS. Discs: Bands: 1. *Traffic noises on cobbles. Mid-close.* 2. *Background of distant factory noises. Steam, metal, throbbing railway engines.*

The creature is crouched beneath a wall under a lamp that suggests we are outside the entrance to a railway station. Two girls stand beside it. They wear the bonnets and costumes of the Salvation Army of 1880-81. They have suitcases and each carries a large tambourine. The one bending over the creature is Janine Mayhew, a slim figure with short, curly hair. The other is Maud Harding, a fair pretty girl.

JANINE: Where do you live? Tell me where you live—we can help you.

The creature turns its expressionless face upwards without speaking. The voice of a man is heard from out of shot and a police sergeant, bearded, enters. (Provincial, not Metropolitan uniform).

POLICEMAN into shot.	POLICEMAN: Now then, Missy, you'll get nought out of that—old soak, we calls 'un around 'ere. JANINE: Where does he live? POLICEMAN: Somewhere down Canal Bank Road. Come on you. (*He gets the creature to its feet*). 'E's mostly to be found round about railway station. (*He looks at the girls' tambourines*). What're you two ladies lookin' for—theatre? JANINE: No, we've just arrived from London. We're looking for somewhere to live. Can you tell us of anywhere—clean, but not too expensive? POLICEMAN: You'd better try Mrs Russell, 12 Albert Terrace—that's where they all go for
TRACK into MS on POLICEMAN.	lodgings. (*The girls have picked up their cases*). You see that road on t'other side of Square? Go down there till you come to cross-roads by theatre, then

	turn down t'right by wall of factory. Along past that, you'll find Albert Terrace up on bank t'left.
MIX CAM 3 Ext. Lodging House door. Night. Close shot on the fan-light of a mean front-door on which in faded paint is the number 12. PAN down.	MIX GRAMS. Discs: Bands: 1. *A soprano singing scales and missing the pitch of top C.* (*In-doors, mid-distant*). 2. *Children playing in street, and factory noises distant.* (*There is the sound of a knocker. After several seconds it is re-peated.* *Inside, a woman's voice (MRS RUSSELL) is heard calling 'all right, all right, I'm comin''*)
The door opens and MRS RUSSELL peers out through the quarter open crack.	MRS RUSSELL: (*a landlady*) Aye, what's to do—what's tha' want? JANINE: (*voice of*) The police sergeant said you could prob-ably give us a room. MRS R: I'm full up. JANINE: (*voice of*) We've just ar-rived. Couldn't you please—if only for tonight? MRS R: What's tha' line—song and dance act, and what's tha' do with them tambourines—kick 'em? I won't 'ave props in my 'ouse, the place for them is theatre.
TRACK back to include JANINE and MAUD in edge of frame.	JANINE: We're not theatricals at all. We're Officers of the Salva-tion Army. MRS R: An' what's that when its at 'ome? I never 'eard of it. Let's ave a look at you. Oh, come on in. I can't stand 'ere freezin' like the tail off a monkey. (*She opens door*).

THE BESPOKE OVERCOAT

by *Wolf Mankowitz*

Produced by *Eric Fawcett*

'The Bespoke Overcoat' was specially written for Television and was so designed that it could be played without scenery.

(ON CAM 2 AS BEFORE)

FENDER: You can't mend the old coat?

MORRY: Please, Fender, do me a favour.

22.
CUT TO CAM 3
2-shot.

FENDER: I can ask? Twelve pound is money.

MORRY rises.

MORRY: (*rises*) Listen, Fender. I break my neck: ten pound for the coat. You got ten pound?

FENDER: I look like a banker? I can save ten pound.

MORRY: So.

FENDER: (*as he starts to put on his old coat*). So I'm going to have made a bespoke overcoat.

MORRY: Bespoke is right.

FENDER: Certainly bespoke. You think I would wear Ranting's rubbish? (*Sits on chair.*)

Hold FENDER when MORRY walks round mattress back into shot L.

MORRY: (*moving DSL and reaching off for patterns.*) What material you like?

FENDER: I can choose material?

23.
CUT TO CAM 2
2-shot.
FENDER sitting Cam R.
MORRY standing behind chair L.

MORRY: (*to* FENDER *with patterns.*) Here, patterns.

FENDER: The grey is not nice for me. The blue is better?

MORRY: (*fingering the blue material.*) Blue is nice. You can wear blue for any occasion.

FENDER: Nigger brown is smart.

MORRY: For a young man.

FENDER: Black is always good.

MORRY: Black is good, but a nice, dark blue is nicer.

FENDER: (*rising, and moving DS of mattress.*) Believe me, Morry, I think you are right. The blue is good—and thick. What a material!

PAN with them slightly to the R.

MORRY: (*down to FENDER.*) I should say. So you can save ten pounds?

24.
CUT TO CAM 1
2-shot.

FENDER: Save? Sure I can save. An old man like me, if I got an overcoat, what do I need? (*Moving DSC to 'B'.*) If I got a bespoke overcoat, what more can I need? (*Exit into darkness DR.*)

FADE DOWN

Scene 5

25.
FADE UP CAM 2
Waist-shot MORRY.

(MORRY *takes out black bread, etc, from his pocket and moves to his chair.*)

MORRY: With a piece of black bread and a herring you can't go wrong. You got in black bread vitamins, nutriment *and* a good flavour from herrings. In the old days, (*Sits*) sometimes six clients a week, all wanting coats, suits, a spare pair of trousers, something. The trade is not good any more. Believe me, if I had a boy I wouldn't let him see a needle and thread. It's a thing of the past. Things are so bad now, you know what I'm doing? I'm making a ten pound coat for Fender. For ten pounds, it's a wonderful coat. The material, the seams. No wind can blow through a coat like this. (*Rises*

MORRY sits on chair.
On beckon TRACK in to CU.

26. CUT TO CAM 3 (As MORRY rises.) Waist-shot.	*and moves DS a few paces.)* Let it blow as much as it likes. I read an interesting thing somewhere. When it's cold, its not really cold. You are hot; that's why you feel the cold. Also you pull in your muscles. That's bad. Fender: his trouble is he's pulled his muscles so far in they won't pull any more. (*Moving DL to exit, as light fades.*) I was always interested
Hold him as he goes out upstage L. FADE DOWN	in science things like this. (*Cross fade to 'B'.*)

THE DISAGREEABLE MAN

An Episode from the Novel

WAYS AND MEANS

by *Henry Cecil*

Adapted for Television by *C. E. Webber*

Directed by *Dennis Vance* and *Barry Learoyd*

Produced by *Ian Atkins*

'The Disagreeable Man' was designed to be played entirely with BP plates. It was specially chosen to show off Television technique on the occasion of the visit of Her Majesty the Queen to Lime Grove Studios.

	VICAR: No thank you.
81. CUT 2-24 *(As before)*	BASIL: (*pouring for the others*) I don't think too hardly of you gentlemen.
	GENERAL: Do you mean that, Merridew?
82. CUT 1-24 *(As before)*	BASIL: After all, I know the way these things happen. Walk into any club in London, and hear what they're saying. Enough material for fifty slander actions.
	GENERAL: Ah, now we're getting somewhere. We very much appreciate your attitude.
	JUDGE: A very generous view.
83. CUT 3-9 CS BASIL.	VICAR: It shows a liberal mind.
	DOCTOR: I entirely agree.
	BASIL: I thank you one and all. But the law, ass that it is, says nothing about appreciating an attitude, or taking a generous

view, or having a liberal mind. Twenty-two respectable . . . yes, I admit it . . . decent and respectable people, have slandered me. Mere tittle-tattle at a party, and yet, it was slander. Should not these people, *because* they are decent and respectable people, be made to pay more than if they were ruffians?

84.
CUT 2-24
Group over BASIL'S shoulder.

VICAR: (*loudly*) How much do you want?

BASIL: Why, Vicar! You don't like listening to sermons? You prefer to preach them?

85.
CUT 3-9
CS BASIL.

GENERAL: (*quietly*) Come along, Merridew. State your figure.

86.
CUT 2-24
(As before)

BASIL: Will fifteen thousand pounds suit you? (*Pause*) Come gentlemen, don't I hear fifteen thousand? Won't someone start the bidding? It's a good case, no flaws in it, guaranteed impregnable against attack.

87.
CUT 3-9
(As before)

What do I hear, what do I hear? No bids? (*Slowly*) I should have mentioned before, that there's a reserve.
(CUT to General, to give Basil time to go to train)

88.
CUT 2-
(As before)

GENERAL: How much, Merridew?

89.
CUT 3-9
(As before)

BASIL: (*off*) The reserve, General? Ten thousand pounds.

90.
CUT 2-24
(As before)

GENERAL: We'll pay.

90A.
MIX 1-24

SCENE 18

NICHOLAS: Basil—Basil.

Railway carriage against BLUE AREA.	BASIL: Ah, there you are. Well, old man, what's the score.
91. MIX 4-24 BLUE AREA	*(Establish London terminus. Voice announces train to Glasgow.)* *(Carriage.* NICHOLAS *making calculations on a bit of paper.)* NICHOLAS: *(calls through door)* Basil! *(Basil appears at door with porter.)* BASIL: Hallo, old boy *(To Porter)* Thank you very much. *(Gives him a pound.)* PORTER: Thank you, sir! BASIL: Goodbye. PORTER: Goodbye, sir! Good luck! *(Exit.)*
92. CUT 3-18 Close 2-shot in carriage.	*(*BASIL *enters with suitcase. Sits and glances at* NICHOLAS*'s paper.)* BASIL: Well, old man, what's the score? NICHOLAS: *(looking at calculations)* Gross profit £10,000. Less my share of £250. And . . . oh, I hope you don't mind this, old boy, I paid the Vicar's £300 for him. BASIL: I don't. That was a nice touch. I don't begrudge that. NICHOLAS: Then living expenses and we lost £500 on the house. BASIL: Tch, tch tch tch tch. NICHOLAS: Had to take the first offer. BASIL: Ah well. Altogether I sup-

93.
CUT 1-24
(As before)

pose we cleared about £8,000.
(Affluent looking lady appears at door.)

BASIL: Madam, allow me!
(BASIL takes her bag and helps her in.)
(Exit Lady to other end of carriage.)

LADY: (OOV) Thank you.

94.
CUT 3-24
RUN MOVING BP

BASIL: A pleasure *(Sits next to NICHOLAS.)*
(Nicholas is staring at Lady.)

NICHOLAS: *(points to envelope.)* *(They both nod.)* Won't last for ever.

BASIL: *(Looking at Lady.)* We can double that in 24 hours.

95.
CUT 1-24
(As before)

NICHOLAS: How?
(BASIL whispers to him.)

NICHOLAS: We can't do that.

96.
CUT 3-9
Close Two-shot (2 Big Heads).

BASIL: Why not, old man?

NICHOLAS: Illegal, old boy.

97.
CUT 1-24
(As before)

(The train starts.)

98.
SUPER 2
Caption THE END.

GRAMS: Music.

99.
MIX 2 to 4
Roller Caption.
(Let it roll off).

100.
MIX 4 to 2
Caption THE END.

FADE ALL

THE SIX PROUD WALKERS

by *Donald Wilson*

Produced by *Leonard Brett*

Here is part of the camera script of the opening of the fourth part of a successful serial. Its complications are self-evident.

4—'The Lilywhite Boys'

Preview:

Cam. 1: (posn. 1 Police Station) Medium CU Sally telephoning.
Cam. 3: (posn. 1 Polly's Kitchen) MS Polly.
Cam. 2: (posn. 1 Polly's Sit. Rm) on Caption Card 'A Television Play', etc.
Cam. 4: (posn. 1 Telephone Box) on Caption 'The Six Proud Walkers'.

HOLD GRAMS OVER BLANK SCREEN FOR SIX SECONDS.	*No Studio* *Sound.* *F/U GRAMS* Theme from 'The Six Proud Walkers' Col. DB3501
1. F/U CAM 4 (posn 1) On Caption Card. 'THE SIX PROUD WALKERS' F/O CAM 4	
2. F/U CAM 2 (posn 1) On Caption Card. 'A TV Play in 6 Episodes by Donald Wilson'. CAM 4 TO TELEPHONE BOX Shot 5. SM CUE POLLY	GRAMS music con.
3. MIX CAM 2 to CAM 3 (posn 1)	Music to b/g. CUE DISC DLO 61243

MS on POLLY. She holds out necklace.

POLLY'S VOICE: Ever seen this before?

Cam 3 PAN R to necklace.

WILLIE'S VOICE: Not that I know of. Do you think I stole it?

CAM 2 to shot 6

MS Martha on stairs.

Cam 3 PAN up to WILLIE's face.

GRAMS music con.

Pv. 1 shot 4—MCU SALLY telephoning.

(on 3 shot 3.)

POLLY'S VOICE: How can you remember about things like stealing when you can't remember who you are?

SM CUE SALLY

4.

F/O DISC

MIX CAM 3 to CAM 1 (posn 1)

CUE DISC

MCU SALLY telephoning.

JOEY'S VOICE: (*on telephone distort.*) You've got the address? . . . Right. Put him on to me. . . .

Cam 1 HOLD telephone as BERTIE walks in replacing SALLY.

(*pause in recording*)

CAM 3 to (posn 2) shot 8

I hear Oscar Lilywhite 'phoned. Tell him I'm working on a cover plan. If he argues hang up.

SM CUE JOEY

F/O DISC

5.

MIX CAM 1 to CAM 4 (telephone box)

MS JOEY replacing receiver. He lights a cigar.

CAM 1 to CAPTION 'One is One etc shot 7

GRAMS music con.

SM CUE MARTHA

6.

MIX CAM 4 to CAM 2

MS MARTHA on stairs.

CUE DISC

Cam 2 TRACK back to 2-shot.

POLLY'S VOICE: Take this and don't let Freddie/Willie

CAM 4 to shot 9 CAPTION SM CUE WILLIE IN	know youve got it. It might bring his memory back.
Cam 2 TRACK in to 3-shot at door. Cam 2 TRACK in to 3-shot at door. Cam 2 TRACK in on POLLY.	*(MARTHA and WILLIE come downstairs and go to door. POLLY opens the door and they go out.)*
7. SUPERIMPOSE CAM 1 On Caption Card, wording in lower half of frame. 'One is One . . . and all Alone'.	GRAMS music con.
8. MIX CAM 2 to CAM 3 (posn 2 Sit Room) CU Clock at 11 o'clock.	GRAMS music con.
CAM 2 to POSN 2 shot 10 F/O CAMS 3 and 1 Pv 4-shot 9 on Caption.	GRAMS music con.
9. On Caption Card. 'Episode 4—The Lily-white Boys'.	F/U DISC Westminster chime 1 o'clock
CAM 3 to shot 11 CAM 1 to posn 2 shot 18 SM CUE POLLY	
10. SLOW MIX CAM 4 to CAM 2 (posn 2) CU POLLY.	POLLY'S SITTING ROOM. NIGHT Continue chime in b/g

SM CUE CIGAR SMOKES CAM 4 to posn 2 (pages)	BOOM 1
11. CUT TO CAM 3 CU JOEY seated settee.	POLLY: Hello, father.
12. CUT TO CAM 2 Close 2-shot seated.	JOEY: Well Polly, where is it? POLLY: Sorry, Father . . . I don't know what you're talking about. JOEY: Don't stall . . . and please don't call me father. . . .
Cam 2 TRACK back to Five-shot JOEY/POLLY seated. FREDDIE enters from behind camera, SALLY to R, BERTIE to L of POLLY. 13.	POLLY: If you don't like the name, you shouldn't have had so many children. . . . (*She looks round and we see that* BERTIE, SALLY *and* FREDDIE *are all in the room and watching her curiously*.) . . . And I see you've brought them all with you. The whole nice clean honest respectable family. . . .
CUT TO CAM 3 Three-shot FREDDIE/JOEY/POLLY, FREDDIE standing L of frame. Pv 2-shot 14—4-shot JOEY seated L of frame.	BERTIE: Except one. FREDDIE: Yes. Where's Willie? GRAMS music off

'1984'

by *George Orwell*

Adapted as a Television play by *Nigel Kneale*

Produced by *Rudolph Cartier*

The production on Television of '1984' caused a sensation. It met with the disapproval of a great many viewers, but was defended in the newspapers, which went so far as to write leading articles about it, and by most of the adult population. Its success was due, in my opinion, entirely to Nigel Kneale's remarkable script and to its faithful interpretation by Rudolph Cartier. Kneale had no easy task. He had to translate a novel of great force and power into terms of dialogue and pictures, and, at the same time, to reproduce its violent impact. As a piece of technical virtuosity '1984' is probably the best script ever written for the Television Drama Department.

F/U CAM Caption NINETEEN EIGHTY-FOUR'. FADE OUT F/U CAM Caption 'By GEORGE ORWELL'. FADE OUT F/U CAM Caption 'Adapted as a Television Play by NIGEL KNEALE'.	GRAMS. Disc: Band: F/U Music.
MIX TELECINE 1. CS Curiously - textured wall: ribbed or made of perforated metal. PAN down wall past notice reading: 'It is ABSOLUTELY FOR-BIDDEN to open this protective cover with-	GRAMS. *Hold music under.* NARRATOR: (*dubbed*) This is one man's alarmed vision of the future . . . a future which, he felt, might with such dangerous ease . . . be brought about. . . .

out specific orders in writing under Section 22/B/YB. Infringement of this Rule is Punishable by death.'

Take in steel cage-like cover hinged to wall. Hands are opening it and we see the heavily-braided cuffs of a high-ranking officer. Inside is a steel casing labelled 'EXTREME DANGER. Open only in STATE OF EMERGENCY. Have you checked your orders?'

The hands unlock combination, swing double steel doors open, revealing a row of internally-lit push-buttons. After a moment's hesitation, hand jabs rapidly at a selected half dozen, then lifts clear.

2, 3, 4, 5, 6, 7.

Stock shots of atomic explosions. The first is very short—only the primary stage. They lengthen progressively.

DISSOLVE TO

8.

Swirling dry-ice smoke.

NARRATOR: (*dubbed*) Atomic war . . . famine . . . revolution. The collapse of a civilization. (*His tone changes.*) And then . . . in its place . . . the formation of a new way of existence. . . .

9.

Slowly bring up through the smoke an almost full-frame portrait of BIG BROTHER. Under it the caption 'BIG

BROTHER IS WATCHING YOU'. It is presented on its own framed hoarding, such as may be seen in Communist countries today.	
PAN slowly off the portrait to (MODEL) view of the Thames at Westminster. We see approximately the same area as in the TV opening signal, but the river has shrunk to a wandering trickle through a weed-grown bed, and of the bridges, only broken arches remain. The Houses of Parliament are burnt-out ruins, but enough remains of the Victoria Tower to identify it, so that we can appreciate the enormous height of the building that next comes into shot.	. . . This, in 1984, is London , , , chief city of Airstrip One, a Province of the State of Oceania.
PAN left to take in a shining pyramidal building over a thousand feet high. It rises in terrace on terrace, with hundreds of tiny windows.	
TRACK in and DISSOLVE TO	
10.	
Closer shot of building.	
PAN Slowly down to take in elegantly embossed lettering across face of	

building 'MINISTRY OF TRUTH'

Not far below come three dark banners, strung across masonry, bearing the Party slogans 'WAR IS PEACE, FREEDOM IS SLAVERY, IGNORANCE IS STRENGTH'

PAN down to windows below.

11.

PANNING shot down on to a single small window in white concrete wall.

WINSTON SMITH is looking out, up at the sky.

CUT CAM

Int Records Dept Ministry of Truth. Day.

GRAMS. Disc: Band:

Background murmur of many people at work in office.

(WINSTON stands looking out of window, one hand resting on the door of a flat case of electronic valves fastened to wall, as if he had intended to open it when his eye was caught by view outside. He turns to case, opens catch; then looks back to window and upwards at sky outside. A slight figure, he is dressed in the dark grey overalls of Outer Party members. Across his back and chest, POW style, is lettered in white: KZ 6090— SMITH W.)

(C.S. Telescreen on wall. This

	instrument has two components: the upper one similar to a large-size television screen of 1954; the lower a large, protruding 'bullseye' lens with a spot of light travelling constantly round the circumference like the rolling pupil of an eye. Both are enclosed in a casing of moulded metal or plastic.
	The electric 'eye' suddenly stops revolving. And the while lens glows. A voice—harsh, flat and metallic—speaks from the telescreen.)
CUT CAM	TELESCREEN: KZ 6090, Smith, W.
	(*WINSTON spins round guiltily.*)
	Face the telescreen!
	(*He does so.*)
	GRAMS. Disc: Band:
	Fade background murmur.
CUT CAM	TELESCREEN: You have been at the window of bay 2 of the Records Department for over eighty seconds. What are you doing there?
CUT CAM	WINSTON: (*confusedly indicating wall-case.*) I came for a replacement valve—for my speak-write.
	TELESCREEN: (*OS*) Your speak-write—ceased to function?
	WINSTON: Yes. Just now.
	(*He opens door of case.*)
	TELESCREEN: You should have notified the fault.
	WINSTON: (*valve in hand.*) Only a moment's work. I've found the right type of valve—

TELESCREEN: (*sharply*) Put it back!
(*WINSTON freezes, then does as ordered.*)
You know it would have been brought to your work cubicle on request.

CUT CAM

(*On Telescreen.*)
This irregularity has been recorded. Return to your cubicle, Smith.
(*Glow in lens dies, and scanning spot resumes motion.*)
(*WINSTON walks forward from window.*)

MIX TELECINE

1.
Door marked 'Inner Party Members only'. It opens as WINSTON comes into shot, and O'BRIEN emerges – a large, burly man in the light grey uniform of the Inner Party. His name and number, O'BRIEN, G. PKY 412 are braided discreetly on the left breast, like medal-ribbons. He watches WINSTON pass with a look of what might be sympathetic amusement. WINSTON catches his eye uncomfortably and goes on.

2.
LS. Records Department: A long narrow room lined with occupied working cubicles. The only window—at the far end—is the one

we have seen, by the open space near the big telescreen. WINSTON walks slowly between rows of cubicles.

3.
CS man in another cubicle looks furtively up from his speak-write as WINSTON passes.

4.
As 3.

5.
A small middle-aged woman, as 3.

6.
PAN WINSTON into his own cubicle. He sits, looks across desk.

7.
Small telescreen on wall behind WINSTON's desk, seen over his shoulder. Its lens glowing.

TELESCREEN: KZ 6090, Smith, W. The repair to your apparatus will be executed immediately.

CUT CAM

(*WINSTON sits still as maintenance man—also in dark grey overalls—comes into shot, flips up casing of speakwrite, and expertly exchanges small valve. The speakwrite, in its streamlined casing, is rather smaller than a portable typewriter, and is supported on a long arm so that it can be pulled towards the operator or pushed quickly back against the wall.*

It has as external features only a mouthpiece on a flexible metal tube, and a metal scoop to receive the paper strip that emerges like ticker-tape from a slit in the side of the machine. On the desk itself; near the side wall is a box-like object with a small loudspeaker embedded in it, a slot and a switch—this performs the opposite function to that of the speakwrite, and audibly decodes messages pressed into the slot. The wall at WINSTON*'s side holds a pneumatic tube for receiving and despatching messages, and a large oblong slit protected by a wire grating —'FOR DESTRUCTION'.*

A calendar shows date—8th April, 1984.

The technician goes. A metal cylinder clatters down the pneumatic tube, and WINSTON *removes and opens it. He takes out a tightly folded copy of the 'Times' and a message — record — a tiny metal cylinder. This he slips into its socket in the machine at his elbow, and switches on. He unrolls the 'Times' and we see it has the same titlepiece as in 1954, but consists only of a small double sheet. The price is 10 cents. From the machine comes a grinding, inhuman voice, low in volume, but clear.)*

VOICE: Correction required as follows: the 'Times' of the 17th

March, 1984—copy sent herewith – contains report of speech by Big Brother.

(*WINSTON finds marked place on second page.*)

He is alleged to have predicted that Eurasian forces would launch attack in North Africa. Please rectify in accordance with facts.

WINSTON switches off speaker. As he turns back to paper, he stiffens. O'BRIEN stands beside him. He has a coarse, humorous, brutal face, and a curious charm of manner.)

O'BRIEN: Good evening. Your technical fault has been put right?

WINSTON: Yes. I'm able to go on now.

O'BRIEN: (*resettles his rimless spectacles and looks over WINSTON's shoulder at 'Times'.*) 'In his broadcast speech last night, Big Brother referred in confident terms to the probability of a large-scale Eurasian offensive early next month. "There is now no possible doubt," he said. "It will be launched in North Africa. Other fronts are expected to remain quiet." ' ,,, An extraordinary error.

WINSTON: (*without expression.*) The speech was evidently misreported.

O'BRIEN: (*also expressionless.*) Grossly misreported, since the offensive in fact came in India.

WINSTON: (*glancing at him.*) South

India. Three days ago.

O'BRIEN: Exactly. Such a careless report. . . .

(*He catches* WINSTON's *eye fleetingly.*)

. . . must not exist.

(*He goes,* WINSTON *looks after him for a moment, then turns to speakwrite, pulls mouthpiece towards him.*)

WINSTON: (*speaking slowly and very distinctly.*) Routine correction to 'Times' of 17th March, 1984, where shown. (*Pause.*) 'In his broadcast speech last night, Big Brother referred in confident terms to the probability of a large-scale Eurasian offensive early next month. "There is no possible doubt." he said. "It will be launched in South India. Other parts are expected to remain quiet."' (*Pause.*) Reprint entire back number . . . and file.

(*As he dictates, the speakwrite emits a steady buzz, and a narrow strip of paper issues from it—not in jerks as from 1954 teleprinter, but in a continuous flow.*)

THE EYE OF A GYPSY

by *Lorca*

Produced by *Christian Simpson*

An example of how far a director can go with a script. On the slenderest of stories Christian Simpson, with the help of music, realistic sound and pictures, built a structure which was purest Television.

SLOW MIX CAM 3 CU Bird-cage. Focus back as Joselito enters tavern. He slowly examines details of the room. He walks towards bird-cage. Holding him in CU crab right past stacked barrels – to lantern which he adjusts to illuminate door-way. Continuing right he arrives at bar.	GUITAR: 'Tavern of The Moor' Mysterioso.
Hearing creaking sound, he swings round towards door—reaching for his knife. Seeing nothing, he turns towards bar and examines knife. His nerves begin to play on him, and finding a glass, he tries the wine-skins, but discovers them empty. CAM 3 He seizes a bottle and succeeds in coaxing	CUE: EFFECT: Door creaking.

from it a few dregs which he hastily drinks.	GUITAR Continued.
Now, keeping his eyes on door, he moves backwards feeling his way along bar. His elbow knocks against some bottles. They totter, and one falls to the floor. Continue crabbing, and PAN down to broken bottle on floor.	CUE: CRASH OF BOTTLE EFFECT
Joselito's feet enter shot. They crunch on the glass, and he kicks away the broken pieces. Hold CU feet. Slow PAN up to hands —then face.	CUE: WATER DROPPING ON POSTER EFFECT
The sound of water dripping works on his nerves, and he looks about him until he sees the torn poster under a high window.	
TRACK in to poster. Savagely he rips it down.	
More composed, he advances to side door. TRACK back holding MS door. He tries to open it, but only his shoulder will budge it. Hold LS exit which he plans to use.	CUE: DOOR CREAKING EFFECTS
He leaves the door slightly open, and moves towards the low window. Crab behind bar	

counter, keeping him in MS. He examines window, and moves over a stool so that he can wait in full view of the window. He waits. TRACK into CU face.	CUE: RAIN EXTERIOR
Suddenly and almost imperceptibly, a fine line is traced across the dirty glass. Joselito half turns towards the window and remains composed. MIX CAM 1 High LS Tavern exterior. A cloaked figure is looking through window. TRACK in to CU hand wiping glass. Joselito is seen inside. He rises and walks towards the bar—as if to receive Pindamonas. The cloaked figure outsides moves left. TRACK left, holding CU hand feeling its way along the wall. As the figure mounts the steps, PAN to hold CU legs. They arrive at the door. One of the feet kicks open the door. The interior is now empty. PAN up the back of the figure. A second shadow appears momentarily in shot—	

A savage blow—and Pindamonas falls forward through doorway. Joselito's face appears looking down at the body.	CUE: DULL THUD EFFECT
CUT CAM 3	
LS Joselito silhouetted in doorway. He looks at the body, and sees a hand lying on the steps, outstretched. He kicks it into the darkness.	
He decides to make a getaway and approaches the open door. He looks about him, then—just as he is about to leave—there is a rifle shot.	CUE GRAMS: RIFLE SHOT
He supports himself for a moment against the door-post, then collapses, sliding down sideways, and rolling over on top of Pindamonas' body.	
A sound of walking feet is heard, which becomes louder.	CUE: FOOTSTEPS ON FLAGSTONES
A pair of spurred riding boots are seen outside the door.	GUITAR ending on Pulsating morendo.
FADE SOUND AND VISION	
F/U CAM 4	GUITAR: Melancolico.
CU solitaire board. PAN up to hold CU Alvarez. He breaks off playing and listens.	CUE: WALKING HORSE
We hear the sound of a	

walking horse. A horse's shadow is seen through the low window.	
MIX CAM 1	
MS Guard . shuffling cards. He listens, then jumps down from bunk and looks into courtyard.	
Focus back to see horse standing – over its back are lying two bodies. Dragging footsteps approach the door.	HORSE STOPS—DRAGGING FOOTSTEPS EFFECT
MIX CAM 4	
2-shot Alvarez and Corporal, who looks haggard and shaken.	
He walks to the form and slumps down, running a shaking hand across his face. Alvarez springs up.	
	ALVAREZ: In God's name, man, what's the matter? Did Joselito fail?